retirementrocks!

LIFESTYLE | RELATIONSHIP | FINANCES

Canadian Boomers Invest in Life

Andrew & Kathleen—
With gratitude
for your support!

Heather Compton
Dennis Blas

2009

Heather
& Dennis

retirementr **cks!**
LIFESTYLE | RELATIONSHIP | FINANCES

Canadian Boomers Invest in Life

Published by: Retirement Rocks!
www.retirementrocks.ca

First Printing 2009 by: Blitzprint
www.blitzprint.com

Logo design by: Twist Marketing
www.twistmarketing.com

Edited by: PTO Editing
www.pto-editing.com

Cover design by: English Designs

ISBN 978-0-9812573-0-3

Contents

Preface

Retirement Rocks! Canadian Boomers Invest in Life is written in the hope that our life experiences might provide some practical knowledge and inspiration for midlife travellers on the same road.

"Investing in Your Life" is the message we bring. We tell our own and others' stories to help, guide, encourage and inspire you to believe that investing in life requires intention followed by action.

We are grateful that the act of writing this book has taken us through our own process of growth, change and learning. You can't write with authenticity about living well in this next life stage unless you make every effort to walk the talk.

The greatest gift the book has given us is a closer relationship. Sharing our views of the project and working toward a common goal has enriched our partnership beyond measure.

Our wish is that reading this book motivates you to enrich your life. Many of the chapters include exercises to help you. The plans and actions involve your lifestyle, relationships, and finances.

To begin, go to "Life Design and Planning" and complete the Gauging My Lifestyle exercise; then review the Retirement Checklist.

We invite you to share your experiences and reactions to our book so that future editions may be enriched through your input.

Heather Compton and Dennis Blas

www.retirementrocks.ca

Acknowledgements

Our deepest gratitude to Kerry and Howard Parsons, our sister and brother of the heart, for your inspiration, wisdom and mentoring, for your support and cherished friendship.

www.centreforinspiredliving.com

Our heartfelt thanks to Barry LaValley for sharing your insight and ground-breaking approach to retirement planning. We wish you continued success.

www.retirementlifestyle.com

A very special thank you to my long time business partner, Gillian Clark and right arm Patty Trimble. I'll always be grateful to the industry, to you, and to our clients for the front-row seat I had into the financial lives of hundreds of families. What a privilege! Our clients taught us so generously and their lessons had little to do with money.

Our love and gratitude to those we treasure: our adult children, our extended families, and our friends and teachers. We appreciate your love, support and life lessons.

Many thanks are due to the helping hands that appeared along the road. To those that have given help and advice, and so willingly shared their experiences and knowledge with us, our promise to you is to pay it forward.

Invest in Your Life

Outlook and Vision
Life Cornerstones
Life List

LIFESTYLE | RELATIONSHIP | FINANCES

Invest in Your Life

Outlook and Vision

*To different minds, the same world
is a hell, and a heaven.*

Ralph Waldo Emerson

*Vision is the art of seeing
what is invisible to others.*

Jonathan Swift

Outlook and Vision

Reality leaves a lot to the imagination.
Create your own retirement reality!

Some of you will recall seeing a delighted, enthusiastic, chair
bouncing and arm-waving Roberto Benigni called to accept his 1999
Best Actor award for the movie he also wrote and directed, "Life Is
Beautiful."

If you haven't seen it yet, you really must! The movie is set in Italy
in the late 1930s. Jewish poet Guido Orefice (Roberto Benigni) uses
charm and wit to win the hand of Dora, an Italian schoolteacher.
They marry and have a child while around them, war erupts. One

fateful day, the Germans arrest Guido and his son and transfer them to a Jewish concentration camp. Dora demands she be taken too.

To protect his son from the grim reality of their situation, Guido tells Giosué that they are on a holiday. He turns camp life into an elaborate charade with himself as the jokester and chief games master, envisioning another, happier, reality. His childlike antics, love of life and family, and his vivid imagination create a grand adventure that delights both his son and the viewer. His persistently positive outlook and his fierce determination to live *only* in the *present* moment create a new reality.

We can be the writer, director and lead actor in our own life. We can construct our own reality for our retirement. Our vision, our life outlook, and an ability to live in the present moment combine to give us the retirement life we dream of.

You are about to be released into your next life phase.

Live in the Present

How *present* are you most of the time? Where does your mind usually try to take you? If you were to stop and notice, would you often find yourself pre-occupied with the past or living in the future?

Ekhart Tolle in his book, "The Power of Now" said, "Unease, anxiety, tension, stress, worry, and *all forms of fear* are caused by *too much future* and not enough *presence*. Guilt, regret, resentment, grievances, sadness, bitterness, and *all forms of non-forgiveness* are caused by *too much past* and not enough *presence*."

Stay present in your life!

Outlook and Vision

Develop a Positive Outlook

How would others describe you? Is your life outlook generally optimistic or pessimistic, positive or negative? Is your glass usually half full or half empty? If you are generally optimistic and positive, these powerful traits will serve you well when retiring. If your life outlook doesn't serve you well, you can take steps to change it.

The power to change our outlook begins with our thoughts or with events and our interpretation of those thoughts or events. Here's how this might work.

thought or event → *interpretation* → *feeling* → *reaction*

The power to change our feelings and reactions begins with our interpretation of events or willingness to change attitudes. Events and thoughts are always occurring in our life. We can control *some* events or thoughts, but *many* we do not control; they just happen. What we can control is how we choose to interpret these events and what we choose to do with some of our thoughts. This interpretation gives rise to our feelings (positive or negative) and then to our reaction to those feelings.

I am reminded of a time when I was stuck in a traffic jam. A truck was ahead of me attempting to make a three-point turn without the space to do so. Traffic was lined up in both directions. It was apparent it would be some time before we would be moving again. The truck driver was hammering his steering wheel and obviously distressed. Every part of his posture showed the state of anger, frustration and anxiety this delay was creating for him. I glanced at the driver behind me. He had opened his sunroof, reclined his seat, and I could hear the sounds of music coming through his window. What a different response to the same event!

Do you ever wonder why others appear to react differently from the way you do when faced with a similar circumstance? The answer is simply that the interpretation they choose is different from yours. You too can choose a different interpretation but you may need to learn or re-learn how to do that. A subtle shift in the nature of the statements you make to yourself and to others will enable learning and change over time. Positive thinking can be habit forming!

When we choose not to be the victim of our habitual responses, we can make change in our life. We can change our physiology because we are all aware of the benefit of slowing our breathing pattern under stress. Laughter, exercise, or even smiling can also change our state. Our other option is to change our thinking. We can do that by imagining ourselves as having other resources, by creating mental visions, or using other triggers such as music. Or we can simply decide to re-frame the experience into something more positive.

Use negative experiences as an opportunity to practise new behaviour. You will establish a healthier pattern of thinking and reacting to life events. There is of course no instant gratification, and it certainly may not always eliminate initial unwanted feelings.

Neuro-Linguistic Programming or NLP promotes the idea of imagining you have an internal control panel. Picture the front of your microwave oven or the dashboard of your car. What on/off push buttons and higher/lower adjustments do you need to have on your personal control panel?

For example, the buttons may be anger, tolerance, happiness, frustration, patience, understanding, or anxiety. Pretend to push and move these buttons and levers in and out or up and down to make attitude adjustments as needed. Do you sometimes need to push the *pause* button or the *emergency stop*?

Create a Vision

Endings give rise to new beginnings, and closing one door opens another. Only by stepping out of our comfort zone and away from the familiar can we make our life more interesting and fulfilling.

What we envision for our lives strongly influences the outcome. Why is this so? Perhaps it's because the stronger our vision and belief in its possibility, the stronger our commitment when we arrive at forks in the road and have to make a choice.

When we think about being retired, it can conjure up all kinds of visions and feelings. At one extreme, retirement may feel like a punishment for failure to accomplish everything we set out to accomplish in our career. Like a jail sentence, some believe retirement should be avoided for as long as possible.

At the other extreme, it might feel like a fairy-tale existence, where all we've dreamed of will come true. Our years of toil and hard work will finally pay off and life will be nirvana. The sooner, the better!

I got together with a former colleague about two years into my retirement and asked him about his plans for retirement. He answered, "I've given it some thought and I'm not ready for the rocking chair yet." That was his outlook on retirement!

We all know inspiring people who are always determined to make the best of any situation. We also likely know some "awful-izers," those who are determined to make the worst of it. What is your outlook towards retirement? Are you an optimist? Are you able to take things in stride? Do you have life meaning and purpose? Do you need to re-discover or re-claim who you are or construct who you'd like to be?

A literal definition of "retirement" taken from the dictionary contains descriptions such as removal or withdrawal from service, moving into privacy or seclusion, to retreat or remove oneself. These definitions are far from true and no longer valid.

Our lives are the result of the choices that we make daily along the way. It is within our power to redefine retirement. *Retirement is an evolving journey without a destination, but with intention of choosing and experiencing life on our terms.*

Choose Your Role Models

Do you know anyone who has retired? What factors have made their retirement successful or unsuccessful? What personal attributes contributed to or hindered their success? How would you choose to be *like* or *unlike* this person in approaching your retirement?

Your retirement life phase may well last longer than your working life! In fact, it might be the longest single period of your life. When I made the decision to leave my career life behind I certainly knew what I was retiring *from*, but did I know what I was retiring *to*? I viewed retirement as a period of my life when I would decide *what* I did, and *when*; as a time when I could make *choices* and live a life that was crafted *for* me and *by me*. Retirement "Life is Beautiful." I chose a retirement that rocks!

To do: Life Design and Planning
            My Outlook and Vision

Outlook and Vision

Invest in Your Life

Life Cornerstones

Heaven on Earth is a choice you must make,
not a place we must find.

Wayne Dyer

Life Cornerstones

This phase of life offers you the possibility to experience life on *your* *terms.* The Boomer generation is not prepared to sit back and be satisfied living the retirement life of previous generations – we want a retirement that *rocks!* The word *retirement* needs to be retired!

It is within our grasp to experience meaning and fulfillment, to be true to ourselves and to renew, regenerate and reinvent ourselves through work, leisure, and learning.

Retirement – the life phase you are about to embark on can be fulfilling and packed with new and gratifying experiences. Through healthy life investment choices, you can create a retirement that ROCKS!"

Retirement Rocks! holds another meaning for us courtesy of Stephen Covey, one of our favourite authors. In his book 'First Things First," he describes a story that one of his associates heard at a seminar. The presenter pulled out a wide-mouthed jar and placed it on the table next to some fist-sized rocks.

After filling the jar with rocks he asked, "Is the jar full?" People could see that no more rocks would fit, so they replied, "Yes!" "Not so fast," he cautioned. He then got some gravel and added it to the jar, filling the spaces between the rocks. Again, he asked, "Is the jar full?" This time the students replied, "Maybe not."

The presenter reached for a bucket of sand and dumped it in the jar, filling the spaces between the rocks and the gravel. Once again, he asked, "Is the jar full?" "No!" the students shouted.

Finally, he grabbed a pitcher of water and filled the jar completely, then asked his audience what they had learned. One of the participants answered, "If you try, you can always fit more into your life." Isn't that what we often *try* to do – fit even *more* into a too full life? "No," said the presenter. "The point is, if you don't focus on the *big rocks* or your *key priorities* **first,** you may fill the jar with gravel or pebbles or sand – something less important – and you'll have no room for the big rocks."

What are your BIG ROCKS?

Each of us needs to redefine our own big rocks or important life cornerstones for this next phase of life. You might for example, believe them to be, your work, relationships, health and well-being, personal activities, and spirituality. And what about money?

Foundation stones, even bigger but less visible rocks, are positive outlook, and life meaning and purpose. We discuss these further in the Lifestyle and Invest in Your Life sections.

Work / Job / Career

We spend much of our life creating and contributing through our work. Using our skill, knowledge and experience in our work satisfies a basic internal drive or need. This drive or need does not go away because we decide to retire.

If we enjoy and gain satisfaction from our work, there is no need to choose a retirement life that does not include work. Perhaps we will choose to work more sustainably or for an organization that fits our values. Perhaps our work role will be unpaid work for an organization close to our heart. "If we love what we do, we never have to work again!"

Dissatisfaction in retirement has been shown to be especially true for those who were *defined* by their work or overly dependent on their workplace title and status. Defining or identifying oneself strictly on the basis of *"do"* and neglecting the *"who"* puts us at greater risk.

Is there more work you want to do in retirement? What are the characteristics of the work? What is your intention, motivation, and need?

Relationships – Significant, Family, Friends, and Community

We interact with others on many different levels on a daily basis and in all areas of our lives. Our relationships are, without question, a cornerstone or big rock in our lives, and they contribute to our quality of life. We call upon close relationships for support and strength during challenging times.

The basic human needs are to share, to be seen, heard, and validated by others, to experience and to feel, to support and to help others and to be supported and helped by them in turn. Neither our laughter nor our tears are as nurturing or as healing when experienced alone as when experienced with someone who is close to us.

Do you have close friends, friends whom you value and cherish, friends that are accepting and supportive of you, friends to grow old with? Do you make a conscious effort to keep in regular touch with friends, to see them and talk to them, know what's going on in their lives for better and for worse? Are you able to spend quality time with your family, immediate and extended? Are all of your family relationships healthy and up-to-date? Is your major love relationship your most important and nurturing relationship? If not, why not? What will it take to change that? Relationship is a renewable resource that requires regular investment!

Health and Well-being

Studies have shown that the risk factors affecting our health are about 30% genetic and 70% lifestyle. Lifestyle choices affect health.

Having health-related goals and taking action to achieve them is critical. If you have good health now, what must you do to maintain it? Will extending your good health require regular planning and action? Can you expect age-related health issues to surface? Good health is essential for you to function well in all areas of your life.

Personal Activities

Have you ever had the experience of asking someone, "So, how are you doing?" to have him answer, "Oh, I'm keeping busy." That's good, but is that what we are looking forward to – keeping busy? There is a big difference between activities that *fill* personal time and those that are personally *fulfilling*.

What are you doing when time disappears? What do you have a passion for? If there are no obvious answers to these questions, ask a different question. Ask from a different perspective in your life, likely when you were much younger and had more freedom. Our interests can get lost or shelved for a time as we become focused and consumed by other things. As we approach retirement, those other things may no longer require the same focus and attention, so it's a perfect opportunity for renewal.

What new activities have caught your eye? Give them a try. If one activity doesn't cut it, move on to the next one. Try a variety of activities – intellectual, physical, social, creative, and solo and group activities. What are you waiting for? What is stopping you?

Spirituality

Our spiritual life is personal. We can choose to add a spiritual or religious dimension to our lives in a variety of ways such as prayer, meditation, yoga, gratitude journals, or an organized religious community. Some already acknowledge the value of a spiritual practice. For others, retirement or another life transition may provide a doorway to exploration.

What about Money?

A high percentage of pre-retirees assume that money is the most important factor of a *successful* retirement. We will simply define "successful" to mean that one is living the life he or she wants and is therefore happy. In other words, he or she could honestly say, "I like my life."

When you talk to people already living in retirement, most place the money factor further down the scale of importance. Preceding money are health, relationships, and meaningful activities.

No one would argue that financial comfort in retirement and the ability to afford a preferred lifestyle are of fundamental importance to "success." However, the source of most of the difficulties and challenges retirees face are not from the financial side of things.

Conclusion

Perhaps a *big rocks* metaphor appeals to you and gives you a useful framework for making choices in your next life phase, or perhaps you view your life as a puzzle. When we work with a puzzle picture, we usually identify the most obvious features and begin by placing those pieces together. Having done that, all the other pieces fall more easily into place.

Puzzles, rocks or cornerstones – what are the most important aspects of *your* life? Are you satisfied with how they line up and fit together?

Invest in Your Life

Create a Life List

Happiness is not a goal;
it is a bi-product.

Eleanor Roosevelt

Create a Life List

Happiness is a by-product of a well-lived life. What do you *want*? What do you yearn for? What have you hoped all your life to see or try? If you have been a spouse, a parent, an only child, you surely have life experience putting the needs of others well ahead of your own. Have you come to a place where you feel it's *your turn* now?

Well, what is it that you want to do, to see, to taste or smell, to try, or otherwise experience before you hit life's exit ramp? What countries do you dream of travelling to? What new hobbies or physical activities would you like to try, even just once? These are wishes more than measures, the longings of your heart, and the visions in your mind's eye. What do you dream of?

There was a movie released in 2008 called "The Bucket List." The premise of the movie has Jack Nicholson and Morgan Freeman (both in their late 60s or early 70s) told they suffer a terminal illness and together they create a list of places to see and things to experience before they pass away.

What would your list include — seeing the Mona Lisa, smelling fields of lavender or fresh cut hay, tasting truffles or caviar, feeling the body rush of crossing the finish line after a marathon?

One of the "Life Lists" that I've been exposed to is by John Goddard (Google his name for inspiration). His life list was started when he was 15 and some of his goals reflect that youthful perspective. He wanted to become an Eagle Scout, ride a horse in the Rose Parade and photograph Niagara Falls. He wanted to swim in Lake Tanganyika, and learn jujitsu and how to fence, and to teach a college course.

If offered the opportunity, what would you say *yes* to? Danny Wallace wrote an autobiographical book called "The Yes Man," which inspired a movie of the same name. One day a stranger on a bus advised Danny to "say yes more." He didn't much like where he was in his life so he decided to see where life would take him if he simply said *yes* to *every* opportunity that came his way. Predictably, he said yes to things he wished he hadn't but he also said yes to things that took his life in new and rich directions. What are you ready to say *yes* to in your life now?

My stepdaughter resisted trying new foods. We asked her to consider saying yes to *just one* new food *a year*. She was delighted to report that she is *years* ahead of schedule! I've said yes to hiking the Grand Canyon, climbing Kilimanjaro, early retirement and learning to play a musical instrument and I hope to say yes to much more.

I'm grateful for the influence of my parents. My mother, a Depression-era Scot, had a cautious fiscal influence that was counterbalanced by the risk-taking entrepreneurship of my father.

My father was a believer that financial risks in pursuit of a life dream were not only acceptable but mandatory. One of his life-list dreams was to start a new ski area in Western Canada. He followed that commitment of his heart but ultimately it did not succeed.

As a family, we teased him that he left his shirt and our inheritance on that hill. Of course, he didn't but I asked him years later if he regretted the loss of the money. He told me, "How could I regret the loss when I had the opportunity to pursue a dream? How many men *ever* get that opportunity?"

I loved my father and respected and valued his teaching that finances or money are a tool designed to operate in service to one's life, and one's life was never meant to be in service to money. My father had a life list in his mind, and he was a good role model for me. When he passed away, he still had many things on his list he had yet to try but he wanted it that way and felt "there's always been something for me to reach for."

What are you reaching for? If you knew that you had only a short time left on the planet – and frankly, that's *all* of us – what would you dare to try? **Challenge yourself to list 100 items.** Don't be intimidated by the challenge. The items on your life list needn't be life changing, unless of course you want them to be.

That may seem a tall order and you'll wonder how to begin. Think in terms of the alphabet. What do you want to try or experience that begins with A – visiting Africa or studying art history? F – more time for family, fishing, or flower arranging? T – travel, textiles, Thailand, theatre? Engage *each* of your senses.

It's through our senses that all pleasure comes. Keep going – it's the key to a rich and juicy life.

To do: Life Design and Planning
            My Life List

Lifestyle

Our lifestyle is the accumulations of choices we make that define how we live. Aligning our choices with who we are, and with our innermost values, leads to a life that Rocks!

Meaning and Purpose
Life Transitions
Health Comes First
More Work or Volunteering
Activities and Hobbies
Travel
Housing

LIFESTYLE | RELATIONSHIP | FINANCES

Lifestyle

Meaning and Purpose

The least of things with meaning is worth
more than the greatest of things without it.

Carl Jung

Meaning and Purpose

It seems that we live in a time when there is never *enough* time. We
live in a time when information and knowledge abound yet
meaningful communication and soulful human connection are
lacking. Technology and other means exist to ease our work and our
lives yet we are unable (or unwilling?) to be still. Far too often, we
are determined to follow the storms, chasing waves with white caps,
avoiding clear skies and the reflective mirror of calm water. Far too
often we are in a hurry and don't know why. We are busy spending
our precious time on what is unimportant while allowing what is
most important to fall by the wayside.

We have become obsessed with mastering minor things. In the end,
we find ourselves enslaved to this pursuit, interpreting the world
and our lives as frenzied. In a sense, we have lost our bearings,
frequently feeling unhappy and harbouring an emptiness that I
suggest is born from an absence of meaning and purpose in life.

What do you long for? What are you drawn to that you are passionate about? What is it that you are excited to do or to experience? Where or what is the source of enthusiasm for you? What kindles the fire in your belly, awakens your soul energy, and feeds your self-worth? What are you interested in and looking forward to every day? What gets you out of bed in the morning feeling pumped and ready to go?

In your responses to these questions lies the answer to the question about meaning and purpose in your life. Do you have life meaning and purpose, and where or in what does it reside? A day in a life without meaning and purpose is like a flower that never blooms. It is more akin to existence than to living, surviving rather than thriving.

A Sixth Sense

The meaning of life is best understood as a concept or as a sense rather than as something tangible. Instead of attempting to explain, thereby implying there is a need to convince someone that meaning is important, let's examine it from a philosophical perspective.

Here are a few insightful and inspiring quotes about the meaning of life from some wise and famous people.

Victor Frankl
"What man actually needs is not a tensionless state but rather the striving and struggling for some goal worthy of him. What he needs is not the discharge of tension at any cost, but the call of a potential meaning waiting to be fulfilled by him."

Invest in Meaning and Purpose

Helen Keller
"Many people have a wrong idea of what constitutes true happiness. It is not attained through self-gratification, but through fidelity to a worthy purpose."

Hannah Senesh
"One needs something to believe in, something for which one can have whole-hearted enthusiasm. One needs to feel that one's life has meaning, that one is needed in this world."

Henry Thoreau
"I have learned that if one advances confidently in the direction of his dreams, and endeavours to live the life he has imagined, he will meet with a success unexpected in common hours."

Stephen Covey
"Whatever is at the center of our life will be the source of our security, guidance, wisdom, and power."

Robert Byrne
"The purpose of life is a life of purpose."

If our primary life meaning and purpose is defined by our careers and our workplace, it is not at all unusual to be unsure and unclear as to what comes next. However, extended uncertainty or a continued absence of meaning and purpose in retirement is a narrow and bumpy road to be on. In this situation, exploration is a worthwhile practical approach to take. Rather than living with a lack of meaning and purpose, experiment with some new ideas by trying them out.

Expectations and Beliefs

You will be much more likely to enjoy exploring new ideas if you are not attached to the outcome. Expectations are a good thing when they are motivating. However, high or unrealistic expectations may not serve you well and in the end can be deflating. Success is achieved in the attempt alone, not in the result. You know the old adage: "It is better to have tried and failed than never to have tried at all."

Our beliefs influence what we are willing (or unwilling) to try. They are the principles that govern our choices and actions. Our true beliefs are the ones when we do what we say we will. When we believe in something, we look for evidence that confirms the belief and we ignore or reject evidence to the contrary. Over time, this causes us to see that belief as a fact instead of what it actually is – *our* belief at a point in time or in a certain situation. Sometimes we will choose to believe something despite the existence of opposing facts.

What you believe is not possible is indeed impossible.

What you imagine is possible, has a real chance.

Lifestyle

Life Transitions

It is not the strongest one that survives,
but the one most responsive to change.

Charles Darwin

Life Transitions

The paradoxical thing about transitions is that they begin with endings and end with new beginnings. The time in between can be very discomforting but we need to view it as the incubation period for an exciting rebirth.

I hope I never lose my ability to remember being a small child and feeling excitement and anticipation about the future. I recall my daydreams of having a motorcycle, driving a car, playing sports with the big boys, learning to catch fish, and on and on. I couldn't wait to shave, believe it or not!

Somewhere along the line, especially when life kicks us hard, it is easy to leave our passion for new experiences by the wayside. It remains our responsibility, as it was back then, to be aware of that happening and to do whatever it takes to pick up our life again. Without those feelings, without that desire, life becomes too humdrum and we can find ourselves just going through the motions.

As we move from one life phase to the next, from childhood to adolescence, to adulthood, from life as a student to building a career, and for some, on to getting married and raising children, we must, consciously or not, make major changes and shifts in attitude.

The Process of Change

We generally react to change in our lives in one of three ways. We get engaged and make change happen *for* us, we sit idly by and watch change happen *to* us, or we wake up after the change and say to ourselves, *"What the heck happened?"* If we are under the impression that entering the retirement life phase will be a quick and easy transition without much change, we'd best re-assess that impression or we may be in for a few surprises.

Any major life change brings with it a transition process. This process has a beginning and an end. Imagine it as a bridge that you need to cross. The bridge has a starting point, an ending point, and some areas of interest along its span. We cannot successfully get from the starting point to the ending point without spending time at each area of interest. How long is the bridge, so we know how long it takes to cross? Typically, we are looking at least at the first year of retirement as a reasonable transition timeframe. There is a risk of stopping permanently along the way because for some reason we cannot or will not move forward.

This transition is mostly a feeling process rather than a thinking process. We are all quite familiar with thinking processes because we deal with those almost every day. The feeling process related to change is something most of us have experienced in the work place, likely more than once. They include mergers and acquisitions, the introduction of major new accounting or human resource systems, new ways to do things, new technology, reorganizations, or a new boss. Sure, a lot of thinking goes on in order to deal with these changes but if we are honest with ourselves, there is a lot of feeling going on as well. The aspects of the feeling process are more or less the same, no matter what the change or when it occurs. The difference, however, is that the feeling process for a major life change such as retirement is so much more personal that each aspect of the process can be more obvious and have a greater effect on us.

The main aspects of the transition process and the areas of interest along the bridge are:

> Endings and unavoidable losses
　　－ bringing feelings of denial, anger, and sadness

> Possibilities and new beginnings
　　－ bringing feelings of uncertainty and confusion

> Moving on
　　－ bringing feelings of acceptance and letting go

Endings create losses

A move into the retirement life phase will inevitably bring endings, some of them positive. The regular paycheque and comfort of a daily routine will end but so will pointless meetings and endless memos. Intellectual stimulation and the camaraderie of your co-workers and business associates may be missing but you will no longer sit in rush-hour traffic and catch planes to places you'd really rather not be. Take a moment to think about the endings you will face.

Identity lost and found

So often in social situations when we meet new people or reconnect with acquaintances from the past, one of the first questions is "So what do you do?" I was initially surprised to find it difficult to say, "I'm retired," at least not without my head down. I felt a strong urge to say what I did in the *past*, for whom, and for how long. I felt that being retired simply didn't cut it. It took a while to come to grips with being proud of a new identity. I needed to let go of defining myself by what I did, instead of telling the truth, instead of allowing *who I am* to be much more important. Any identities we choose (or are asked to adopt) that are from *external* sources are always temporary. Forget for a moment about what we do or did. Who are we? Do we know or have we been on autopilot for so long we've lost touch?

For much of our lives we found ourselves singing someone else's tune and marching to a beat that wasn't ours. That's not necessarily the problem because for some periods this may be unavoidable and done by choice. The actual problem is that we don't take the time to become aware of what's really going on. We end up on "autopilot." Awareness helps us to get off autopilot, spend the time and find the space necessary to remind ourselves of who we are.

How would you describe yourself? What do you like and/or dislike most about yourself? What is most important to you about you? How would you describe your life? What do you like and/or dislike most about your life? What is most important to you? What is most abundant in your life? What is missing or absent? When do you feel content, comfortable and safe? When do you get sad or angry? How do you feel most of the time? What are you doing or thinking when you are feeling your best or your worst? What are you thinking about when you are excited and having fun? What do you love to do and when do you do it? What do you want most for your life? What do you dream about?

Possibilities bring uncertainty

Gordon Livingston, M.D., in his book "And Never Stop Dancing," states, "Happiness requires an ability to tolerate uncertainty."

Until we sort through the possibilities ahead of us and make some decisions about what comes next, we will face a period of uncertainty that comes with any life transition. This can often be the most challenging stage.

Many of us have held tightly to the illusion of control and certainty in our lives because it felt safe to do so. The alternative, which is closer to reality, can cause us to feel frightened and anxious. Until we are willing to let go of this illusion of control, we are held back from moving on with our lives in a way that allows us to thrive. It can be a tremendous relief to realize that it (whatever *it* is) isn't in our hands and it never was in our hands.

If you find yourself *reminiscing* about the *future* or *making plans* for the *past*, you have it backward and it's time to move along! Remember the song by Elton John "Cross the Bridge or Fade Away."

Moving On

Getting stuck can happen at any age. My son had just completed university and was now in the real world looking for employment and acceptable living accommodations in the big city. He found himself agonizing over *every* choice he was faced with, over *every* decision he needed to make to move forward. He would get stuck judging whether those decisions were good or bad, right or wrong. The problem is caused by thinking in black and white and looking at *every* decision as needing to be *the* good one and *the* right one. The powerful implication is that all other options are bad and wrong.

So often in life, the issues are quite grey. In an effort to move his decision making along, I said to him, "When you come to a fork in the road, take either path. There will be other forks." Little did I realize the effect those few words would have on his outlook. He later had a ring engraved with *"Take either path."*

It is a lesson, I think, for all of us as we move forward into this retirement life phase. Experiment by avoiding the use of the words right, wrong, good, bad, never, and forever. Avoid using them in your thoughts and in conversation with others. Notice whether it makes a difference to your outlook and to your willingness to make choices and decisions.

We must trust the evolution of the process, both internal and external. Perspectives will change as we cross the bridge. The transition process is an evolution not a revolution. New insights are gained; goals once set can be altered along the way.

Heather's Story

At 50, I retired from a career I loved and clients I cared deeply about. Both my children were away attending university. My long-time business partner and dear friend moved to Spain. My husband had already been retired for 6 months. My 20-year-old son was grappling with the question of what he wanted to be when he grew up. I was in no position to help him with that question, because I no longer knew who I was or wanted to be! Every role that had previously defined me was gone – vice-president, financial advisor, business partner, mother. I was in TRANSITION.

Transition is that uncomfortable place in-between saying goodbye to *what was* and waiting for or seeking *what's next?* We all have experience of endings and new beginnings. Remember negotiating the new terms of engagement when you first married or wondering what the heck had happened to your carefree life once you'd had a child? Perhaps you have experienced the breakdown of a marriage or long-term relationship, or the death of a life-partner or close friend or family member. For some, a milestone birthday is enough to start the transition process.

We pour so much of our energy into our work or other *roles* that when we finally stop, we just need to catch up and relax, take life a little more slowly, and be patient with ourselves and with our partner. A new life is unfolding.

The decision to leave our work-centered life and move into a new life phase is a major turning point. It presents a wonderful and oftentimes frightening opportunity to re-evaluate who we are. We need to redefine our roles, carve out a new place for ourselves and re-assess all that we hold as important.

We all know of others who wanted to avoid the discomfort of transition. Think of the guy who runs off with someone half his age or the woman who chooses surgery or contracts a high-priced designer to redo the house. We can run but we cannot hide because eventually we must do the work of re-examining who we are and what we want from life. We are compelled to re-evaluate purpose and meaning. We're called to craft a *new* life.

Lifestyle

Health Comes First

*It is health that is real wealth and
not pieces of gold and silver.*

Mahatma Gandhi

Health Comes First

How many of you have a negative view of aging and of the term *senior*? Why do we value aging in a *wine* yet disdain it in the wine *drinker*? The Boomer generation will undoubtedly come up with a new term we feel better about, but the truth is we can never be young again and we are entering life's final chapters. On my 50th birthday, a friend pointed out to me that I had arrived at the life stage where the look forward was not as long as the look back. Thanks for cheering me up!

We do have to age but we don't have to get old!

It was Satchel Paige, an American baseball player, who once said, "If you didn't know how old you were, how old would you be?"

Dr. Thomas Perls, a leading U.S. longevity expert, says 30% of how we age is influenced by genes; about 70% is lifestyle and habits. He has developed an Internet quiz (livingto100.com) that calculates life expectancy based on family history and personal habits. Perls has produced a long list of characteristics that those over 100 share. Among them are a sense of humour and a zest for life which he says helps to manage stress and keep blood pressure in check. His information suggests smoking cuts lifespan by seven to ten years and obesity knocks another six years off. Eating lots of vegetables and fruits, as opposed to red meat and fast food, can add eight years. Apparently, regular flossing adds a year!

Perhaps the good news is that we can influence life expectancy and it is increasing. Perhaps the not-so-good news is that all of the extra years are tacked on at the end of our lives. Medical science can keep us *alive* but we are responsible for seeing that we *thrive*! The World Health Organization describes health as a "state of complete physical, mental and social well-being and not merely the absence of disease or infirmity." That requires caring for all aspects of health – **economic, physical, emotional, mental and spiritual well-being.**

Exercise for half-an-hour a day; eat a diet rich in fruits, vegetables and whole grains (and low in fats and refined sugars); spend an hour a day in stress-reducing activities such as yoga or meditation and you can slow down aging, according to a study by the Preventative Medicine Research Institute. This healthy lifestyle spurs a 29% boost in the activity of an age-defying enzyme called telomerase that usually declines with advancing years.

Imagine your body as a vehicle that you can't replace. What would you change to ensure its proper functioning for the next 30 to 40 years? If we look back 10 years from today what will be different? Roll up your sleeves and prepare a vehicle maintenance schedule!

Start with the exercise "Health Comes First" in Life Planning and Design. Add just five items to Health Comes First.

Invest in Health

Economic Health

Economic health has an obvious effect on physical well-being and health in parts of the world where access to the necessities of life such as clean water, food, housing and health care are at stake. Thankfully, in North America, even our most economically disadvantaged citizens are helped by social safety nets subsidized by our tax dollars. Makes you proud to be a taxpayer, doesn't it? We deal with ways to enhance economic well-being in the finances section of this book.

Physical Health

Changing poor lifestyle habits, improving our diet and nutrition and regularly engaging in moderate physical activity will all pay big health benefits. Do you know what you need to do now (and are doing) to feel good and function well physically as you get older? Do you need to change any existing habits that you know affect your health? Is your good health a priority for you because you want to live a long and healthy life? If you are overweight, you already know you should lose a few pounds; if you are a smoker or drink too much you know you need to stop. If you've never darkened the door of a gym, it's time to get a membership! If you haven't been to the doctor for scheduled maintenance, that regular check-up, you know it's time!

A 2007 survey by Health Canada, Stats Canada and the Canadian Institute for Health Information found that 56% of the Canadian men surveyed were either obese or overweight. That was 16% more than the women surveyed. In North America, obesity causes 300,000 premature deaths each year! It is second only to smoking as the leading cause of preventable death. High blood pressure, high cholesterol and Type 2 diabetes are all consequences.

Our Doctor and the Health Canada food guide are two very good examples of where to go to increase our knowledge in this area. Canada's food guide to healthy eating is available on the Health Canada web site (healthcanada.gc.ca).

Depending on metabolism and exercise, women only need between 1,200 to 1,700 calories per day and men 1,800 to 2,200. We need to burn about 3,500 calories to lose just one pound of body weight. Online resources offer useful databases of nutritional and caloric information for generic and brand name foods. Check out calorieking.com, thecaloriecounter.com and eatracker.ca. Go to caloriesperhour.com to see how long you must exercise to justify eating that treat. Successful dieters claim recording what they eat in a food and activity journal plus regular weigh-ins are the key to their success. Try eating meals from a salad or luncheon-sized plate instead of a full-sized dinner plate.

Discipline, of course, is not available from a web site, nor is it an automatic by-product of gaining knowledge. The discipline comes from *us*. It comes from setting a goal and being personally committed to that goal.

Another threat to our mental and physical health as we age is stress. It includes the level of stress we experience and how well we handle it. For some of us, much of life's stress arises from something that has happened or is happening, something that we have little if any say or involvement in. We fret endlessly over it rather than getting on with the job of dealing with the consequences or of just letting it go. To worry is to put ourselves at the mercy of forces outside of us, which we cannot control. "Worriers" have perfected the art of imagining how something can turn out badly.

The single best way to manage stress is through physical exercise. Aside from stress management and improving outlook, it is well known that regular physical exercise provides many other benefits, including improved fitness, flexibility, strength, cardio-vascular health, and weight management, all increasingly important and not to be taken for granted as we age.

Small initiatives can have great payoffs. According to the American College of Sports Medicine, effective health gains can come from just 10-minute bursts of moderately intense physical activity accumulated throughout the day. In studies exploring long-term weight maintenance, a common element of success was 200 or more minutes of moderate intensity exercise per week or just 30 minutes per day.

A walking program is a great place to start. "Step into a Healthy Life" is an initiative promoted by Australian health authorities (10000steps.org.au). Ten thousand steps is the recommended daily step goal for a healthy adult. A good pedometer to measure those steps can cost as little as $20 and focusing on that daily step goal is a great way to stay motivated to walk the stairs or park the car farther from the mall entrance or to juice up your vacuuming. Right! Nothing juices up vacuuming!

Walking and jogging are good for your heart but don't do enough for keeping body fat down and preserving muscle as we age. Our workout plans need to include a mixture of resistance exercise like weight training and cardio-vascular conditioning. Stretchy exercise bands are an inexpensive fitness accessory and great for toning muscles, especially when you don't have access to a gym while travelling. There is a whole body range of exercises you can use these for. Borrow several exercise CDs from the library and try them out. Buy only the ones you like.

One of the first abilities we lose as we age is our sense of balance. Many of my clients had to give up golf or hiking as they aged because their sense of balance was impaired. Add a wobble board or inflated fitness ball and balance exercises to your program now. Standing on one foot while on the phone will strengthen your core and improve your balance.

As we age, other aspects of physical health come into play. The Canadian Hearing Society notes 46% of middle-aged people have some hearing loss. Have a hearing test *and* regular eye examinations because both glaucoma and macular degeneration are more common in older adults. See healthcare professionals regularly to have blood pressure and cholesterol levels checked. If you are not able to find the time in your busy life for managing nutrition and physical exercise, you can be assured that you *will* find the time for ill health.

Mental Health

We all become aware of the evidence of deterioration in both body and mind by the time we've reached our forties, fifties, or sixties. Perhaps the evidence is nothing more than stiffer joints first thing in the morning or walking into a room and not remembering why we went there in the first place.

An article in Nature, a top science magazine, featured comments from seven prominent neuroscientists on the use of chemical "cognitive enhancers" to help enhance memory and learning. Several drugs are now being tested in humans that may help stave off age-related memory declines. Soon we may all remember where we left the car keys!

The field of mental health includes dealing with the challenges of brain chemistry imbalances and related disorders such as depression, through a focus on medication or therapy. Your doctor's personal advice and monitoring trumps any research, but in a review of 29 studies, lead author Klaus Linde, M.D. found the herb St. John's wort relieved major depression just as well as a standard antidepressant.

What about retaining or enhancing mental acuity? We all need to work our neural pathways so they don't shut down any faster than they do naturally. Most of us think of playing bridge or doing crossword puzzles or Suduko math puzzles as good mental acuity solutions and they are! Studying a new language, taking up a musical instrument, reading and remaining socially engaged are others.

New research shows that the key is to "change it up" regularly just as you would with a weight workout so those mental muscles remain constantly challenged. Don't get lazy repeating tasks you have already mastered.

Playing video games may help to improve memory, reasoning and multi-tasking ability in older adults, according to a study by Dr. Arthur F. Kramer at the University of Illinois. Gaming Company Nintendo has developed Brain Age games for the Nintendo DS hand-held game system, based on research by a Japanese neuroscientist. These games keep us on our mental toes by randomly changing the challenges and increasing the complexity of the tasks as we start to catch on. Nintendo has also developed the Wii gaming system that comes bundled with a games package called Wii Sports for virtual tennis, baseball, bowling, boxing and golf. An extra purchase gets you the Wii Fit game with a balance board for yoga and other exercises. While you won't become an elite athlete or even raise your heart rate or fitness level much, these do get you off the couch and keep you mentally stimulated.

We have a friend who is reliving his rock star years through a game called Guitar Hero. Game marketers have found a way to bring together grandma and the teenage gamer in the family. In fact, many seniors complexes are buying the Wii Fitness programs as a way of keeping seniors both physically and mentally active and socially engaged!

Strong social ties and frequent human contact may be the key in preventing dementia. A large study by Harvard School of Public Health appeared in July in the American Journal of Public Health. Researchers showed that people 50 and over who have an active social life would experience half the rate of memory decline as the least socially inclined group. Participants scored quite high on social integration if in the past year, they had volunteered at least one hour a week, had contact (phone call, e-mail, in person) with one of their parents and one of their children once a week or more, got together to chat with neighbours once a week and were married. Becoming a social butterfly is good for your mental health!

Retired or not, leisure is important. We need leisure in order to re-charge ourselves and sometimes to act as a distraction in our busy and demanding lives. We use leisure to experience excitement and fun, or to just rest and reflect. Be cautious in retirement that leisure does not become the major life component because leisure may lose its value and attractiveness when it is the focus in our life rather than the getaway. There is a big difference between "time-filling" activities and the "fulfilling" activities that we look forward to. A lack of stimulation affects our mental and emotional outlook, and then our physical health and well-being. The real danger is allowing the "not having to do anything" to turn into "not having anything to do." Eleanor Roosevelt said, "Never be bored and you will never be boring."

Exercising the mind seems continual and automatic when we are in the workplace as we learn new jobs, use new technology, and keep pace with the changes that come at us. In retirement, we need to choose to challenge and rejuvenate our capabilities on a regular basis.

Emotional Health

Emotional health means having a full emotional range, including laughter and joyful, exuberant play, plus relationships or connections. Some believe joy and sorrow are located on the same tap and that if we don't allow ourselves to experience one, then we can't fully experience the other one either. Our work life trained many of us to mute our emotional responses, sometimes to the detriment of our personal relationships. Retirement is a time of emotional freedom when, like singers extending their vocal range, we have the freedom to test other responses in the emotional register that add to a richer life.

Our most important emotional resource is our attitude. Many schools of thought suggest we are in charge of our attitude. You don't need to be a curmudgeon unless you choose to be! Even acting as though you are gregarious makes you *feel* more outgoing, which is linked to a more positive mood. Research at Yale University found that, even at 50, just *feeling* upbeat about getting older is linked, on average, to seven more years of life.

The field of Neuro-Linguistic Programming or NLP advocates creating a Mental Control Panel or "mother board." The philosophy is that all of us have the resources to effect change and choose what to be. Imagine if you could move a control in your imagination and that control was connected to a "joystick." What if you were about to say something you know you shouldn't so you hit the emergency stop button instead? What would it be like if we could dial up our enthusiasm, optimism or determination whenever we needed to?

The concept of the control panel puts you in the driver's seat. Dennis and I both have an internal control called tenacity that we can call on to gut things out when our tanks are empty. In fact, that mental control lever got us to the top of Mount Kilimanjaro!

Spiritual Health

Considering spiritual health may mean adding yoga or another regular spiritual practice, such as prayer, or joining an organized religious community, studying meditation or going on solitary retreats. Regularly stepping through the doors of a house of worship may slow your progress to the pearly gates according to a University of Texas study.

A women's resource centre in our city recently hosted a class called Laughter Yoga. See laughteryoga.org for more information on the founder of laughter yoga and laughteryoga.ca for information on the group in Canada. They claim that practising laughter exercises enhances brain chemistry, improves mood, reduces blood pressure and decreases stress! Wow – emotional, physical and spiritual health all in one class.

Our spiritual, emotional and relationship health may be enhanced through a daily gratitude journal. At bedtime, just before putting out the lights, reflect on at least three things that you are grateful for in your day and note them in your journal. They might include a grandchild's smile, the sound of a beautiful symphony, or a fresh loaf of bread. We focus on what we *have* in our lives instead of on what is missing.

Examining our interior life and life's "big" questions is a natural part of the aging process. A spiritual practice may serve you in finding your life's purpose, tuning in to your own internal wisdom, and living your life as a sacred journey.

Summary

Medical science can keep us alive but we are solely responsible for keeping our own bodies and minds in the best condition possible. The truth is that we are all aging and no matter the effort we make to improve our health, we simply can't turn back the clock. Even cosmetic surgery holds back the hands of time only so long. Perhaps our objective shouldn't be to pretend we're younger than we are but to choose to age into a collector's classic edition!

We all wrestle with the paradox that we want to live a long life but we don't want to get old. My mother regularly reminds me that getting old is not for wimps! Healthy aging includes coming to terms with the reality that we aren't here forever. The awareness that we are *all* headed to the exit ramp can cause us to live more fully in the moment and not waste even one moment of this precious gift. Our greatest defence is to learn to live and take pleasure in the here and now.

To do: Life Design and Planning
My Lifestyle - Health Comes First

Lifestyle

More Work or Volunteering

The best medicine that I have had is the knowledge that I had a job to do.

Albert Schweitzer

We make a living by what we get, but we make a life by what we give.

Winston Churchill

More Work or Volunteering

What does *retirement* really mean? What about the fundamental human needs that work fulfills?

Those who continue to be active in some type of meaningful activity or *work* during retirement are generally more successful, happier and more satisfied than those who are not so engaged. To reach this state we generally need to widen our view and accept a broader definition of what *work* might entail in this next life phase. Perhaps our *work* includes a role as a volunteer, a new career in an unexplored area of interest, a return to student life, reduced hours at our present place of employment or with a new employer, a role as a consultant, or self-employment and creating a small business enterprise.

Some will choose to continue working for reasons other than financial, and will make sure the work does not consume or dictate their life. A *life plan* for this phase means creating a balance between contributing to society, learning, playing and working. We will learn to work more sustainably. Those who work because they need the financial resources will examine ways to add more choice to their work life and roles.

Needs Met by Work

In addition to the need for financial security, comfort, or to add "life's extras," several other needs are satisfied in whole or in part by our work.

Meaningful Pursuits – the sense of purpose that work provides and the satisfaction, challenge and recognition that results.

Daily Routine – the routine and structure that work provides on a daily basis.

Identity and Status – important measures that include our sense of self-worth, power, authority and personal competence, our job title or our position in the workplace and larger community.

Belonging / Community – the feeling that there is a place in society that welcomes us, a community that we belong to of like-minded others with common pursuits, social connections and friendship.

Intellectual stimulation, creative expression, job "perks" such as health care and administrative staff and personal growth are all needs that our work life may fulfil. The basic nature of these human needs means it is critical to be aware of the degree to which they are or were being met through our work life. Choosing to retire and leave the workplace does not eliminate the needs nor will it diminish their importance. We will just need to find new ways to meet them.

Dennis' story

I worked for 35 years in Information Technology. Much of that time was spent in management roles for larger companies. I woke up one day to a work life that felt quite empty, unsatisfying, and rather meaningless. That didn't just happen that particular day, did it? My children were through university and essentially launched. They were almost off the payroll. The question staring me in the face was "Why am I doing this work? Is it just for the money? Is it healthy for me? Is there an alternative? I quit my job. I left my 35-year career. Was that frightening? Did I have doubts and second thoughts for some time? Yes!

When I made the decision to end my long-term career at the age of 54, I never for a moment considered that I would not work at all. I had a plan as to what I was going to do, how I was going to do it, and when I was going to begin. My reasons for wanting to work were not financial, at least not primarily.

Building things and doing small renovations was my hobby during my career years and a life-long interest forged and encouraged by my father when I was small. It was an escape for me, good for me physically, and therapeutic in terms of my mental outlook – a great stress release. Over the years, I improved my skills and gathered my own collection of tools, including some treasured tools I inherited from my father.

I became a jack-of-all-trades and capable with carpentry, electrical, plumbing, and tile setting. You guessed it! My plan in retirement was to continue this type of work, to have fun with it, and to make a few bucks at the same time. Obviously not too sure of my new identity, I ended up buying a new black suit, a pickup truck and a new toolbox months before I left my white-collar downtown job!

I had several friends who knew of my intentions and they all had long lists of projects. I was off and running at full steam ahead. Before too long, I found myself working evenings and weekends, and doing maintenance work that I truly did not enjoy. This had never been part of my plan. Heather said, "You didn't quit your IT career to work longer hours for far less money!" She was absolutely right. I had great difficulty saying "No."

I learned to say "No," and I learned to take on only the work that I enjoyed. I reserved free time for other things. I became very selective whom I did work for, the projects I took on, and the timeframes for completion. I had a plan and modified it along the way. I knew the road I was on and was able to change lanes.

Here's another personal example. About two years into retirement, Heather and I decided to diversify our investment portfolio by holding assets in residential real estate. We started with limited knowledge and no experience. In order to increase our knowledge and to understand what we wanted to accomplish, we enrolled in a real-estate agents' training program. It was a little intimidating for me because I had not written an exam in over thirty years but I passed! In fact, we both did but Heather got the higher mark, as I am affectionately reminded! We held an agent's license for one year and purchased several revenue properties. We were trying a new idea and we stumbled, learned, and challenged ourselves. It was a growing experience with purpose.

Invest in Work and Volunteering

Did either of us foresee these things happening when planning for retirement or when entering retirement? No. Opportunities showed up because we made space in our lives and we were open to giving it a go. Why not?

Therein lies the difference for many of us, between working *before* retirement versus working *after* retiring. We were now in charge, doing what we wanted, when and how.

Heather's story

Let me ask you, "If you were in the driver's seat, would you work five days a week? Would you work through all twelve months of the year? Would you work a full or long workday? Not many would, in my experience. Do you love aspects of what you do?

You know that when you are engaging in something that you love, there is a sparkle in your eye and a spring in your step. You also know when you aren't in that sweet spot, you are like a high-powered car operating in a lower gear. You growl and the gears grind!

I retired because I wanted *more* of what I love to do. I continue to present retirement seminars and write books because it's part of what I love to do and I can choose my time.

If you have not left the workforce yet, you may not wish to imagine a time when you will *ever* willingly choose work again. Fair enough! We often need to close one chapter of our life before we open another. I had worked since I was 15 and had raised my boys as a single parent while developing my career. I was tired. I needed to rest and rejuvenate, play, read, workout, putter in my garden, and have lunch with friends. When I cleaned all my closets and cupboards, Dennis supportively suggested that I might need to look for *"more"* in my life.

More in *your* life may mean more work or it may not. Retirement and *life* is an evolutionary business that calls for an awareness of our changing needs, strengths, interests and passions. Many of you will work again, but you will be more careful in your choice.

Could use the Money

Recent economics have made many think they need to return to work or put off the retirement decision.

The American Association of Retired Persons reports that 33% of all retirees re-enter the job market within two years of retirement. Some of those retirees resume working for the extra income, some for the other needs that work fulfilled.

Having a phased-in retirement with continued cash flow for several years can *greatly* reduce the size of the retirement pot you will require, versus planning for a *full* or conventional retirement. Reduced hours and cash flow may let you retire sooner than you thought.

If you believe you could work in sustainable ways rather than your present frantic pace, you might well consider some form of work well into your 70s. The Finances section offers several ways to calculate your retirement requirements.

Recalculate the *pot* assuming part-time work supplies perhaps $10,000 or $15,000 of your cash flow requirements for another five or ten years. Now consider the possibilities.

Invest in Work and Volunteering

Consider the Possibilities

Before you rush out and take just another "job," consider what else might be possible. Perhaps you will stay with the same employer but re-negotiate the terms of your employment, or you will leave them and come back in a consulting capacity with greater flexibility. Work seasonally or on a project basis. Perhaps your existing work role would continue to fit you after a sabbatical and a change of perspective, or if a flextime schedule was possible or you delegated away some aspects of the job. Consider taking a role with a non-profit or an educational organization, trading off salary for contribution. An internship or volunteer opportunity may lead to paid employment. A brand new role with another employer may be the solution. Could you go back to school full or part-time and become qualified in something you always dreamed you would pursue? Try something new on for size, as Dennis and I did.

At the age of 55, Grandmother Doris Maron sold everything she owned and hit the road on her Honda Magna 750 motorcycle. She put 120,000 km on the bike on an around-the-world trip that took her three years. Now back home, she still loves to ride and has written two books about her adventure. At 60, she went back to work, for a while anyway!

Our good friend Bill quit work at 60 after a long and successful career. He still loved his work but he wanted more free time and he had a vision of the job he wanted. He wanted to work Tuesday, Wednesday and Thursday, from 8:00am to 3:00pm. He wanted a minimum of 8 weeks off a year, he only wanted to use a specific set of skills he really enjoyed using and he didn't want to manage people any more.

At a few initial interviews, he was told what he wanted didn't exist but within six months he was hired into the exact job he had designed for himself. His skills were valuable! There are many more options and alternatives available to Boomers these days than in the past as businesses are prepared to be flexible to retain experienced people.

A Budding Entrepreneur?

The opportunities for self-employment and entrepreneurship are endless! Employees don't have many tax deductions but tax deductions are useful! I buy books and subscribe to magazines that interest me. Because I legitimately use them in my work, they are a deductible business expense. In order to stay current on events in the market, federal budgets and changing pension legislation, I need my Internet service and newspapers, all deductible business expenses.

Is there a way for you to create meaningful work and deductible business expenses doing what you love to do? Be sure to keep careful track of business revenues and expenses. The CRA wants to help small business but they aren't interested in subsidizing your hobby!

Expense Deductions

The types of expenses you can deduct depend on your business. Canada Revenue Agency has several useful publications available online (cra-arc.gc.ca Forms and Publications) or visit a local office.

IT-514 Work Space in Home Expenses
T4002 Business and Professional Income
RC 4070 Guide for Canadian Small Business

Invest in Work and Volunteering

Jeff's hobby was to rebuild classic collector vehicles in his spare time. He subscribed to car magazines and he liked to travel to car shows, all of which he had to pay for with after-tax income. In retirement, he decided he would work on a few more cars and sell them to create income. He needed to attend the occasional car show and subscribe to car magazines to do research for his business. Those expenses may be deductible business expenses! Canada Revenue doesn't dictate how much you have to earn, but if you have deductible expenses, you have to have an *expectation* of earning a return from the business.

Karen loved quilting, but how many quilts does a person need? She had already made beautiful quilts for friends and family. In retirement, she arranged with a shop to sell her quilts on consignment. That allowed her to write off some of the expenses associated with her quilting business.

Nice Work!

We were buying garden pots at our local farmers' market one day and struck up a conversation with the fellow operating the stand. He and his wife were retired and now travelled around Mexico every winter to buy inventory for their new business. The market is open just Thursday through Sunday and operates from late May through the end of September. Nice work! The key is to redefine work on *your* terms.

Volunteer Work

Lending our skills and talents to others in a volunteer capacity can give form and structure to our days, give us a purpose and focus, and for some, a soul-satisfying means to give back to our community. People who volunteer at two or more organizations have a 44% lower death rate than those who don't do any charitable work according to the Buck Institute for Age Research. They claim there is a "biology of compassion" that boosts antibodies to a level comparable to exercising four times a week.

You might choose an unpaid role with a professional association or a spiritual or religious organization, a community service role or an involvement with coaching and athletics. Tutor newcomers, read to children or deliver meals to seniors – name an issue and there will be an organization that needs your time. For some, the volunteer position will become a demanding full-time role in a cause they feel passionate about; others will lend an occasional helping hand or find a way to add volunteer time to their other roles. The key will be to find the right fit.

Cora Marie Clark found her role as Toothena the Tooth Fairy. Formerly a dental hygienist, at 52 she now consults to dental practices across North America. Closer to her heart she has self-published a children's book and started The Tooth Fairy Children's Foundation (theToothFairySpeaks.com). She fundraises to support teaching children in Kenya about dental care.

Brian has eased back to a part-time role in the financial services industry. He spends one afternoon a week stocking hampers at the local food bank. He and his partner Julie act as event ushers and ticket takers for local theatre groups several times each season and in exchange see the plays free!

Wayne helped with various activities at his Rotary Club while he was working full-time but now retired; he has a central role organizing the club's annual fundraising campaign.

The Volunteer Canada (volunteecanada.ca) site is a great place to start looking for your role. They provide links to local volunteer centers across the country where opportunities are listed. Local offices act as matchmakers and the site has a questionnaire that will help you determine a role you are suited for.

Some look for volunteer opportunities that will take them overseas. Check out Canadian University Services Overseas (cuso.org) or Canadian Executive Services Overseas (ceso-saco.com). Both are typically looking for highly qualified professionals but other organizations take on volunteers in other capacities.

To do: Life Design and Planning
                My Lifestyle - Work and Volunteering

Lifestyle

Activities and Hobbies

*The quality of a life is
determined by its activities.*

Aristotle

Activities and Hobbies

Many people plan to start new activities *once they retire*. Although the
types of activities vary considerably, the good intentions are similar.
Even basic physics tells us *a body in motion stays in motion*. If you aren't
actively engaged in hobbies or other interests *now*, what will change?
What are you waiting for? Why not get started?

Author Ernie J. Zelinski says, "It's difficult to experience pleasure
reminiscing about things you haven't done."

Retirement is a time of greater freedom to choose and try *new*
activities and interests. That requires us to redevelop our willingness
to be a beginner. Zen master Shunryu Suzuki instructed his students
to approach their meditation practice with Beginner's Mind. He
said, "In the beginner's mind there are many possibilities; in the
expert's mind there are few."

Memory Lane

Think back to when you were a kid. After hours at the skating rink you *finally* mastered a hockey stop, played your first band concert to an audience, or learned to dive into the pool. In those moments, you became a "master of the universe!" Young children aren't afraid to admit to themselves or others that they don't know how to do something. They are willing to look dumb, make mistakes and risk failure and embarrassment. Because of beginner's mind, they go places and try things we won't, and their lives are richer for it. Most adults have forgotten how to be a beginner!

Somehow, bumping along life's road we learned to colour only between the lines or not to draw too much attention to ourselves or make fools of ourselves. Others have been in long training as perfectionists and if we can't display a certain level of competence right out of the gate we say, "That's it – I quit."

Being a Beginner

Have you been a beginner at *anything* in the last 12 months or less? What was it that you began? Was it hard? Did you stick with it long enough to attain a level of enjoyment? Notice I didn't say competence – I said enjoyment. There is absolutely no rule that says you have to stick with something that you discover you don't enjoy even if you *are* good at it. One of life's paradoxes is that "easy" paths end up being difficult and the difficult paths end up being easy. Learning to play the flute is hard, achieving yoga postures is hard, studying a new language is hard but each time you are a beginner it makes the next beginner experience easier, and the pleasure of accomplishment and the ways in which you enhance your life make life *easier*, richer and juicier!

Not trying anything new or not moving out of your comfort zone feels "easy" at the outset but your life gets harder – it has less colour when there are no challenges or new things to talk about or look forward to. I'm reminded of a story of a man who decides to go back to school at age 70 and his friends tell him, "For heaven's sake, by the time you're finished you'll be 80." He replied, "I'll be 80 anyway – might as well learn something new along the way!" Learning new things takes concerted effort, practice and a willingness to face challenges and be humbled.

One of my "Life List" objectives is to try a *"new to me"* activity *every* year. As the years go by, that may get harder to do but simply having that as an intention has led me to try out all sorts of interesting possibilities. I've competed on a dragon-boat racing team, flown a glider, tried painting classes – my list goes on. I'm grateful for Dennis' inspiration and his willingness to "play." Together we have taken up or shared rollerblading, snowshoeing, a real estate course, squash, kayaking, couples programs, snorkelling, writing a book, co-presenting seminars, weight training and ballroom dancing, not all successfully. He excels at squash but I gave it up. It turns out he is a capable dancer but I'm rhythmically challenged! Oh well. Success isn't my measure but living a full and juicy life and embracing new growth, possibilities and challenge is my goal.

Perhaps your partner isn't as willing to play as mine or you don't have a partner. Don't let that get in your way. We cherish the friends we have developed, together *and* individually, who will share pursuits with us. In fact, some activities I simply prefer to pursue alone. You can join book clubs, painting groups, go hiking, skiing, and join other clubs to find like-minded people. Universities and colleges often offer continuing education calendars filled with opportunities to try new experiences and they accept solo registrants.

Timing is Everything

Through health issues, physical limitations, infirmities or simply lack of interest, some of us will become less active over time. What activities do you need to do sooner rather than later? If you want to begin weight training, is 90 a good age to start, or should you move up the timeline? If you want to learn to read music and play a musical instrument, can it wait until you are 70? Some of you will be aware of family health issues, perhaps vision problems such as macular degeneration, which may mean that painting, needlework and photography ought to be pursued while you still have good eyesight. Knitting or woodworking can help to keep arthritic fingers mobile; those joints that we use, we don't lose.

We all need outlets for our creative expression even if we don't see ourselves as artists. If you have been a logical, sequential, analytical or left-brain thinker all your life, what liberation it is to discover those aspects of yourself that are more right-brained, random and intuitive.

Trial and Error

Inspire yourself. Write down in your "Activities and Hobbies" (Life Design and Planning), the physical activities, sports and hobbies that you would like to *try*, that you'd like to do *more* of, or that you'd like to *bring back* into your life. Which new activities have caught your eye? Try them and if they don't "take," move on and try another. Some of these will be *passive* leisure activities such as watching sports; others will be more *active* and engaging pursuits. Some activities or hobbies you will pursue *solo*, others you'll share with your *partner* and still others mean that you will join a team or gather a *group* of friends.

Try to vary activities between several different types such as intellectual, physical, social and creative to meet all areas of your well-being. You will appreciate activities that allow you some solitude, or cheering in the stands as a spectator. For variety, you will want to be actively involved. Try activities for emotional and mental health that have you socially engaged and intellectually challenged. Try physical activities that help to manage weight and contribute to a healthy cardio system, or activities such as meditation and yoga that feed you spiritually. The activities that *fill* personal time, like watching television, are very different from those that are personally *fulfilling* such as hiking with friends.

Inspiration

I collect newspaper articles, magazine stories and pictures of mid- and later-life role models who inspire me. There are loads of *famous* mature role models like golfer Arnold Palmer and ex-president Jimmy Carter but I prefer stories about *mere mortals*, like me. One article in my file features great-granny Peggy McAlpine tandem paragliding a day after her 100th birthday. She reported the experience was far superior to bungee jumping, which she did at the age of 80!

Sid Ingerman still looks good in Lycra! He started running at age 68, became a tri-athlete at 75 and this past season completed four sprint triathlons before turning 80. A sprint triathlon combines a 750-metre swim, a 20km bike ride and a 5km run. Most of us would be happy with one of the three!

Jim Martin took up slo-pitch and hockey as a 66-year-old retiree. Still a goalie at 86, he doesn't like to tell people how old he is because they get preconceived notions about what he can do. When asked how he would know when it was time to hang up his skates he said, "When I wake up in the morning and see my name in the obituaries!"

I take great pride in my Uncle Ethan. He was still winning downhill ski races at 88! He teases people by saying that the reason he won was that he was the only competitor left in his age category.

Some of us lack a vision about the activities, hobbies or sports we'd like to try! Pick up books such as "How to Make the Rest of Your Life the Best of Your Life" by Mark Victor Hansen and Art Linkletter. Art Linkletter, who most of us remember from "Kids Say the Darndest Things," is still writing books at 94! This is a wonderfully inspiring book with endless ideas of how to get engaged and involved.

See what you might choose from the list below or use it as inspiration to create your list.

A – Create art, study archaeology, acting
B – Coach baseball, walk barefoot, start a business, learn bridge
C – Join a club, take a canoe trip or a cruise, do cooking classes
D – Take dance lessons, daydream, have a date
E – Teach English overseas,
F – Fly a plane, fishing, go to flea markets, build a fort
G – Time with grandkids, gardening, set a Guinness Record, golf
H – Study history, go hiking, ride a horse, hot air balloon ride
I – Invent something, play an instrument, surf the Internet
J – Jump rope, join a club, journey to new places
K – Knit mitts for the homeless, make a kite
L – Study languages, write letters to friends, join the library
M – Learn to ride a motorcycle, climb a mountain, have a massage
N – Go to night school, do nothing
O – Attend the opera, play the oboe, seek opportunity

P – Adopt a park, play ping-pong, plant a tree, paint, play cards
Q – Question something, go on a vision quest, enjoy the quiet
R – Restore furniture, study world religions, run, read, rollerblade
S – Learn to sail, swim, sing, go snorkelling, sponsor a child
T – Tennis, teach, tai chi
U – Go to university, play the ukulele, umpire a basketball game
V – Volunteer, use your voice, join a choir, grow vegetables
W – Write a book or poetry, make wine, join a walking club
X – Play the xylophone
Y – Rent a yacht, say yes more often, ride a yak, visit the Yucatan
Z – Visit a zoo, study Zen thought, go to Zanzibar

To do: Life Design and Planning
My Lifestyle - Activities and Hobbies

Lifestyle

Travel

*We wander for distraction, but
we travel for fulfillment.*

Hilaire Belloc

Travel

Yes, you will *still* take vacations when you retire! The opportunity
and intent to travel ranks high on the priority list for many retirees.
Turn to the Life Design and Planning section and list your top five
travel destinations in your "Travel Plans." Don't share this list with
your partner until you have both completed your own lists.

Not everyone *wants* to travel post-retirement. I had many clients
who had their fill of travel in their working life and wanted nothing
better than to stay put and many were never bitten by the travel bug.
For others, physical health and affordability crimped their travel
plans. Can you imagine what else might get in the way? Believe it or
not, once you've been there and can check those important
destinations off your list, you won't continue to travel in the same
way.

Rather than jetting off to exotic locations, many clients were happy
to fly to Regina to see the kids or to Disneyland to share a holiday

with the grandchildren or to Victoria to enjoy some rounds of golf or camping in the mountains. They chose these over seeing the Great Wall of China a *second* time. After some foreign travel, others felt there was no place like home and they put away the suitcases permanently!

One of the trips on our life list was to climb Mount Kilimanjaro. You need a good set of legs in order to climb Mount Kilimanjaro, so we knew that trip needed to come sooner rather than later in our retirement life. Traveling to Hawaii could perhaps wait until we're 80, if good fortune holds, but trips that depend on our physical capacity need to move up the ladder!

Go back to your travel list again with a new perspective. Do you need endurance or other physical attributes like strong hiking legs or sailing or riding lessons in order to make that trip? Which trips need to be "sooner" and which can be "later?" Map out some specific travel plans.

What *type* of travel is each entry on your list? For example, do you prefer activity or adventure based trips, visiting friends and/or relatives, an exotic vacation spot, winter get-aways, or volunteering? In each case, will you travel alone, with a partner, with friends, or in an organized tour group?

If you are working, how many weeks of holidays do you have? Cast an eye on that travel list again. Could you take some of those trips while still in the workforce? Your cash flow is good, your health is in great shape and the good news is you are still on the planet.

Regretfully, some of my clients hit the exit ramp before they ever had a chance to take some of those trips. They needed to stop saying, "When I retire I'm going to…"

Invest in Travel

Follow your latest fascination. There are cooking trips, travels that feature remarkable gardens, train trips and wine tours. One of my clients liked to travel to a new place each year to compete in a 10k run and see the city. Another reclaimed his life as a "groupie" and travels to see his favourite performers in person.

Wonders of the World

The Egyptian pyramids are the only surviving structures from the original list of seven architectural wonders of the world. The other six are long gone. You can surely win a trivia contest if you are able to name them! Choosing world wonders has been a continuing fascination over the centuries and a new Seven Wonders of the World campaign was begun in 1999 by Swiss adventurer Bernard Weber. The campaign began with over 200 nominations from around the world and over 100 million votes were cast to determine the winning seven new wonders. Weber's hope was that the world could be united by a shared pride in our global cultural heritage. Introduce yourself to the winners at new7wonders.com and cast a vote in his new contest for the seven wonders of the *natural* world.

Exploring UNESCO's list of World Heritage Sites (over 800 sites) even as an armchair explorer is a wonderful way to see the wonders our globe has to offer! Books such as "1000 Places to See before You Die" provide further inspiration.

What Did You Say?

Ever get to that other country and regret that you couldn't speak the language? Most travellers are eager to try at least a phrase or two. Many of the travel guide companies, such as Lonelyplanet.com and Frommers.com publish a series of phrase-finder books that give you a mix of practical and social words and phrases. Chatting with the locals, or trying to, has enriched *all* of our travel experiences and lead to some great interaction. Before we travel somewhere new we try to obtain a list of the most essential words – hello, thank you, please, yes, no, I don't understand, where's the toilet? Night classes and "For Dummies" DVDs can also be helpful.

Speakshop.com is a website that uses video-conferencing software to enable people to learn Spanish in the comfort of their home from live tutors in other countries. The best part is the philanthropic edge. Teaching for this service allows the tutor-entrepreneurs to set their own rates and schedules and students select a one-on-one tutor based on their bio and interests.

Hostel Living

The hostels of our youth are not the hostels of today. They too have grown up! Instead of dormitories and communal showers, many now offer private rooms with en-suite bathrooms. Some offer language or tango lessons, on-site bars, cinemas and spa and massage services. Hostels are no longer the sole domain of backpacking youths.

The emergence of more upscale accommodations is attracting more mature customers and families too. Hostelworld.com is one of the biggest and most comprehensive Internet booking sites for hostels. They rate thousands of hostels worldwide based on character, staff, fun, security, location and cleanliness.

The most popular hostels are in top destinations such as London, Rome and Paris, with growing interest in Eastern European and Asian destinations.

Home Exchanges, Rentals and "Points"

As travel budgets shrink, more travellers will look to reduce costs through home exchanges or vacation rentals.

Seniorshomeexchange.com and other home exchange sites offer members an opportunity to do a vacation exchange of their home. Some sites charge an upfront fee to list your property; on others a fee is payable when an exchange is arranged.

Sites such as Vacation Rentals by Owner (vrbo.com) or Vacations Abroad (vacations-abroad.com) offer travellers the comforts of home, often more affordably than a hotel room. As the properties usually have a kitchen, you also save money on meals. Make sure you ask for pictures and check references.

My Scottish blood always has me looking for good value. To help you make the most of travel rewards, several good websites offer tips on accumulating, redeeming and using your memberships to get free or discounted travel upgrades. The place to start is Rewards Canada (rewardscanaca.ca), with its focus on Canadian points.

Voluntourism and Edutourism

Among the biggest trends in the travel industry are combining a new destination with volunteer activities or educational pursuits. There are some great ways to combine a love of travel with a want to contribute.

First, enjoy the beaches in Thailand and then spend a week helping in an elephant orphanage or help to build a school before your trek in Nepal.

For those looking for your own "Raiders of the Lost Ark" experience à la Harrison Ford, sign up for an archaeology dig. The Biblical Archaeology Society lists many excavation projects that need volunteers; in many cases, no experience is required. Like similar volunteer experiences, you cover your own travel costs and it is customary to contribute to food and housing costs also. For information: digs.bib-arch.org.

Pamela was looking for a meaningful way, beyond the standard "coming of age party," to mark a significant birthday. She and an 80-year-old co-volunteer ended up celebrating their milestone birthdays on a Habitat for Humanity build in Hungary. Contact habitatforhumanity.ca for details.

Elderhostel.org is a U.S. based travel-education program offering literally hundreds of programs in virtually any subject you can name. Order their free catalogue or search the website. Dennis and I have enjoyed kayaking programs offered through our local university.

Also becoming hugely popular is multigenerational travel when grandparents take their children and/or grandchildren on vacation. Cruises and sun holidays to all-inclusive resort properties are a good way for families to get together should you have the financial resources to make it possible.

A Great Packing List

Wherever you go, it's important to have what you need without over-packing, especially as airlines are charging generous over-weight baggage charges. Dennis, thankfully, is a "systems" guy. He maintains valuable packing lists for our various styles of travel.

A kayak trip, a day hike, a longer backpacking trip and a couple of weeks at our time-share in Mexico all require different packing essentials. His lists mean we don't forget things. For packing lists and helpful travel hints, check out onebag.com and travelite.org.

Travel Insurance

A few fortunate retirees will continue to have medical coverage when travelling through a continuation of the company benefits from their former employer. Private travel medical insurance can often be purchased on a per-trip or a year's contract basis.

If you take several trips per year and you can qualify for an annual policy, this is often the way to go. Save those receipts! Your premiums may qualify for a tax credit as a medical expense. Many credit card companies are including travel insurance as part of the marketing appeal of their premium credit cards.

Regardless of the source of the insurance, read the fine print carefully, particularly the information related to the dollar limits and age limitations on coverage. Many policies have a relatively low ceiling on payouts per incident. Some policies will ask you to pay for services up front and claim later. Answer the health questionnaire carefully and accurately or you risk invalidating the coverage.

Even if your travel takes you within Canada, you likely need travel insurance coverage. Out-of-province medical expenses are only covered to the maximums of the home province's schedule and these schedules vary considerable across the country.

Dennis and I are backcountry hikers and backpackers, so costs to be evacuated from remote areas are not part of *any* province's coverage and can be high.

"Away" at Home

Many cities offer "get away at home" programs that show all there is to see and do right in your own backyard. We have attended slide programs offered by travel companies, our public library and the university that are *almost* as good as being there. We own a set of Planet Earth DVDs that provide a view of the world's wonders without leaving our home.

Even as I age or lack financial resources, I will continue to find ways to see the world. Perhaps it is the legacy of my seafaring grandfather who spent his youth in the merchant marines, but I hope never to lose my fascination with the sights and the history of the world around me!

To do: Life Design and Planning
              My Lifestyle - Travel Plans

Lifestyle

Housing

*A house is a home when it shelters
the body and comforts the soul.*

Phillip Moffitt

Housing

How do we decide where we are going to live in retirement and when should we make the move? We will likely consider selling our present home if it costs too much to maintain or becomes unaffordable, or if we require the capital to live on. We might consider selling our home if we want to travel for longer periods and have a lock-and-leave arrangement so we don't worry about the house being checked, the yard being maintained and the sidewalks shovelled, keeping insurance coverage current, and so on. We may simply want to downsize or move to another location or country. A large percentage of us will simply stay put.

Need a Home

It's important to look at the needs a home fulfills for us. My home is an important social hub for entertaining friends and family. One of the things on my housing wish list may always be a decent-sized dining room. For some people, a hobby room or entertainment center is important. Some view their home simply as an investment and are quite willing to move when they need to call on the dollars.

Dennis and I have considered alternatives but he needs a separate garage or workshop to putter in for some time yet. An apartment condominium with an open parking area won't fit our needs. We still have two adult children living with us so sufficient elbowroom is still a requirement. Eventually, we may want a low-maintenance lock-and-leave home, but not yet; there may be an in-between solution, such as a townhouse or condo.

It is important to look at the needs your home is required to serve and to open your mind to all the different ways those needs might be served. My clients have chosen many interesting options. Some of them got wrapped up in marketing campaigns that depicted a fantasy life in a faraway exotic location only to discover that what they really wanted was proximity to family and long-standing social ties. Some of these things you won't know until you take the leap and try it out.

John has kept his inner-city Calgary home. He rents it out to help pay his living expenses and mooring fees for his sailing boat. He isn't ready to resume life as a landlubber yet but when he is, he plans to sell the boat and return.

Big Changes

My business partner, Gillian, and her husband Len sold everything here in Canada and moved to Spain. Family worried that they might not like it there but Gillian's attitude was "I won't know if I like it until I try it, and if I'm just a visitor I won't be fully a part of the experience I'm looking for. I need to be there lock, stock, and barrel in order to experience Spain in the way I want to experience Spain.

If it doesn't work out, I'll return." Obviously, there could be financial and other consequences of a decision of that magnitude but Gillian brought her engineer's mind and training to the cost-benefit analysis. I believe we also have access to personal wisdom that guides us to the right thing to do.

Another friend and his wife moved to Costa Rica and built a home and restaurant there, cutting their ties to Canada. They love their life there but are clear about the tradeoffs they have made and, in fact, recently bought a small condo in Canada to have a home-base for visiting friends and family.

One of my clients had health concerns and wanted to pursue an RV lifestyle while he still had the good health to do so. He did not have the financial resources to hang up his hat and retire for good. His plan was to sell his condo, use the proceeds to buy an RV and head off for five years. At the end of five years, it was his intention to buy a new condo, sell the RV and get a job. He asked for my thoughts.

I'm sure you can see the downside to the plan. He planned to sell an appreciating asset to buy a depreciating asset. Sometimes in life we are called to step off the curb and just hope to heck the pavement comes up to meet us. I said, "If you are asking for my *financial* blessing, I can't give it. Tell me from a life-giving perspective if you believe it's the right choice." He did.

Ian brought together the best of all that he was looking for. He liked skiing and golf but his first criterion was a congenial pub. He tells me he is leading the life of Riley! He and Jan retired to a small community in central BC selected specifically for its pub and access to the amenities they wanted. In the winter, he is a volunteer "liftie" loading skiers on the ski lift in the morning and skiing free in the afternoons. In the summertime, he's a course marshal at the area golf course. Again, he works free in the morning, and plays golf free in the afternoon. He tells me his life just could not get any better.

Check it Out

If we are thinking of living somewhere else, perhaps we should visit that location in different seasons. I love the sunshine in Calgary and I love the climate and activities that Victoria offers, but will I get sufficient sunshine? I won't know that until I spend some time there.

Clients have upsized, downsized, moved to different provinces and different countries, lived on barges and had long-term home exchanges. Almost anything is possible. Those who have done their homework have looked at access to cultural and entertainment activities, education opportunities, nature, recreation facilities, personal growth opportunities, healthcare facilities, work and volunteer opportunities and the people they love and want to spend time with. They have considered the cultural flavour and types of people, the geography and affordability and climate.

Dennis and I know we are "city mice." We value walking to restaurants and coffee shops and love theatre, the symphony, museums and dance programs. We enjoy going to the gym, riding our bikes and hiking in the mountains. We want access to all these things and proximity to friends and family. The trade-off for us is a difficult winter climate that we plan short-term escapes from. Friends prefer the solitude and serenity of a country setting.

Communicate with others who've gone through the process. Does the location you are considering fit your lifestyle? What are the resources in the area – medical care, a hospital, activities that you like to engage in, museums, art galleries, libraries, good fishing, good golfing, and so on? Do you know what "musts" are versus "nice-tohaves?" Do you have a plan B if plan A doesn't work out or are you prepared to go with the flow? Does your significant other see things in the same way? Is compromise possible or can you live in one location and then another?

Many hope to retire abroad or at least spend some part of the year elsewhere. Do some homework. Visiting a country is not the same as retiring there. Seek out the community you are likely to live in and rent for a few months. Take a realistic look at finances. Mexico, Costa Rica and Belize may be cheaper to live in but factor in costs such as airfares, additional healthcare expenses and communications costs. Consider the taxation and estate issues if you plan to own property elsewhere. Will you retain ties to Canada or become a non-resident? Understand the financial and other implications of your choices.

The Government of Canada offers publications and website information on visas, regulations and laws (voyage.gc.ca). Follow the links to Retiring Abroad. The Canadian Snowbird Association is a not-for-profit group that offers group rates on travel medical insurance and links to other sites (snowbirds.org). Country specific sites are also popping up to attract your retirement dollars (explorecostarica.com and meexpatriate.net).

To do: Life Design and Planning
              My Lifestyle - Housing / Lifestyle Priorities

Relationship

Connection with others is as important to the well-being of our soul as nourishment is to our bodies. Relationships are our foundation.

On Your Own
Life Partners
Friendships
Parenting
Three Generations

LIFESTYLE | RELATIONSHIP | FINANCES

Relationship

On Your Own

I celebrate myself,
and sing myself.

Walt Whitman

I am in relationship with life
... I love my life.

Suze Orman

On Your Own

Reality alert – by chance or by choice, a high percentage of us will be on our own at some point on this retirement journey. Singles will include those who have clearly made a lifestyle choice to be on their own, those wishing for a partner but not willing to settle and those alone through relationship breakdown or the death of a partner.

Recent Statistics Canada figures show that living alone is a reality for almost *40% of women* at age 65 or older. This is not a female-only planning issue but ladies, *pay attention*! Many women turn over the financial side of retirement planning to their partners not realizing that, ready or not, it *will* become theirs to deal with. The critical issue for *all* of us to consider is what our life might look like should we be on our own. How should we plan for the future with this in mind?

Role Models

Positive role models are important for *all* of us, whether solo or partnered. It is always instructive to see examples of other's lives working well. It gives us an idea of what is possible, and for some, it will be an incentive to reframe our own life view. For some singles, reframing their life view will become a well-practised art. They won't look through a viewfinder and think "alone again," but will say "alone by choice" or "blessed solitude." Those with a long and chosen experience of single-hood see it as a choice and likely don't require this skill of reframing.

Those who find themselves *unexpectedly alone* – the widows, widowers or those experiencing relationship breakdown – may need to alter their outlook on life alone.

Finances

The tax system gives no tax breaks to single retirees. *All* Canadian retirees qualify for the personal exemption and may, in addition, qualify for other tax relief through the age credit, pension income credit and deductions for RRSP contributions. One area of tax relief that *may* have greater potential for a single is the range of deductions available for operating a business in your home. There is every chance that the percentage of the home you direct to business use could be larger.

The tax system's newest and most valuable innovation, income splitting, is of no value to you and, of course, there is no spouse or common law partner to qualify for the spousal exemption. You may, however, qualify for an "equivalent to married" exemption for a dependant child, grandchild, sibling, parent or grandparent. The dependant must be under 18 or dependant by reason of mental or physical infirmity. Review the chapter on tax strategies or see the Canada Revenue Agency website.

Concerning money and finances, the differences for a single person may include lower net worth and reduced living expenses. With lower household income and total net worth when compared to many two-income families, the reach for financial independence may take longer and be more challenging for singles to achieve. Most will need to be more cautious and focused on saving and spending priorities both before and during retirement. There really is no magic. It's crucial to spend less than you bring in and that will require some creativity on your part.

Estate planning and life insurance can certainly be simpler for a solo, although this is likely *not* the case for single parents. For a single person, it is critical to give someone Power of Attorney over your legal and healthcare issues should you become incapacitated and unable to act. Government benefits such as CPP and OAS will add to your resources and it may be that some will qualify for extra income assistance. Be sure to read the relevant chapters for further details on these sources of income.

Housing

Two can't *really* live as cheaply as one. One person bearing the full burden for mortgage payments and home maintenance led to some creative solutions on the part of my single clients.

Sue purchased one side of a duplex and had a legal suite put in the basement. During her working life, the rent from the suite helped her accelerate her mortgage pay down and in retirement she accepted reduced rental income for *some* cash flow with the balance paid *in kind* with maintenance duties.

Other clients were willing to share their home with student renters and one woman we know took in short-stay ESL students travelling to Canada to study English. Some singles value condo living or communal living arrangements to lessen the maintenance burden.

Work

Many of my single clients continued to work, usually part-time, often into their 70s. For some, this was financial necessity but for others, it was because they enjoyed the intellectual stimulation, social connections and feelings of self-worth their work brought them. Many made career moves to more sustainable work or to roles with feel-good organizations, often for less pay but greater feelings of contribution.

Travel

It has never been easier for singles to travel solo. Travel companies offer trips in all budget ranges and many do not require a singles supplement, especially if you indicate your willingness to share accommodation. Elderhostel and other groups offer tours directed at mature travellers, if that is your preference.

Dennis and I met Pat, a 50-something American living in Britain while on a trip to Egypt. She was on her own with no extra payment because she had indicated her willingness to bunk with a roomie but no other single females signed up. I talked to her about her experiences travelling solo and she indicated she loved travel and her trip satisfaction was directly related to the dynamics of each group. She loved Canadians and asked each travel provider how many Canadians were signed up before she registered!

Tony, a 60-something guy, shared a Grand Canyon hiking trip with us. He was delighted to be tent sharing with our adventure tour guide, Barb.

Health

Singles, like their partnered counterparts, need to put a focus on *all* areas of their health and well-being. Some areas can present challenges; for example, meal planning and cooking for one can be a chore.

During my years as a single parent, I was strapped for time *and* financial resources. A girlfriend and I would get together for cooking nights. Armed with four or five recipes and a bottle of wine, we would cook batches for the table and batches for the freezer. We enjoyed a visit, saved money and ate more nutritiously.

For the kitchen or time challenged, many supermarkets and speciality food retailers sell packaged meals for singles. These can actually be less expensive than regularly throwing away produce you haven't used.

Particularly as we age, we may develop health issues and have no one nearby to call on for assistance. Services like Lifeline operate across Canada and will, for a fee, monitor and answer calls sent on your personal alarm, notifying family or emergency services (lifeline.ca).

Relationships

Immediate and extended family relationships may continue to contribute to or even form the core of your life in retirement. Some will not have family members to call on but even those who do will, for reasons of geographic or emotional distance, look to non-family relationships for emotional support.

Friendships, in particular the close ones, can be even more important when you are on your own. This is as true before retirement as it is while retired. Perhaps these close supportive friendships are already in place and are a solid life cornerstone. Some of these friendships may be with work colleagues and will readily survive the retirement life transition.

Some of us will move to new communities or will have other reasons to want to expand our friendship pool. Book, hiking, swimming, or dance clubs, education programs or recreation courses through your local community college or city programs, library, museum, or health club memberships can all serve as a starting point for new relationships.

I recently read about a grassroots initiative called conversation cafes. Their mandate is to bring together interesting people looking for community and conversation. You can join a group or start one in your area. Details on the concept and guidelines can be found at conversationcafe.org.

To do: Life Design and Planning
My Relationships (Friends, Family and Friends)

Relationship

Life Partners

Shared joy is a double joy.
Shared sorrow is half a sorrow.

Swedish Proverb

"There are times when I don't quite know what to do with
you, but heaven knows what I would do without you!"

Life Partners

The most valuable asset that couples share is not their home or their
investment portfolio but their relationship. Retirement can bring
your relationship to a new level and allow you to create new
dimensions in your life partnership. It can also be a risky time
because it brings forward new stresses and strains and uncovers
some old ones you've left buried. Typically, retirement makes your
relationship *more* of what is was prior to retirement.

If you share a harmonious, supportive and loving relationship,
chances are that the greater freedom, shared activities and closer
proximity will make the relationship even richer. Proximity and time
may make a challenged relationship even more challenged, and
there's no time like the present to change that!

Dennis' View

My marriage with Heather is my second try. We teasingly refer to ourselves as "Retreads!" Heather and I are each other's mulligan! We joke there will be no third time at bat; the only possible option left may be murder!

I was divorced in 1993 after 20 years of marriage. I prefer to view divorce as an event in one's life and a very significant event, there is no question, but I do not consider divorce as a state of being. I was single, then I was married, then I was single again and eventually re-married.

The ending of my 20-year marriage has been the worst and most difficult experience of my life so far. It was also one of the greatest life gifts I have received. I say this without remorse, regret, judgment or blame directed at others. I say this about me. The emotional shock and trauma and the deep pit of grief served to teach me so much. It has allowed me to rediscover my core self. My choice was either to wither or move on in my life with a different and healthier outlook, taking nothing for granted; knowing by then that relationship is our foundation. I did the best I could in my first marriage, and as a result of its ending, I can do better now.

Let me clarify something very important. I am not suggesting that in order to be where I am today, my marriage had to end. Couples go through some tough times in their relationship. The luckiest ones are those that are able to survive and even flourish through those times, learning and growing together, nurturing each other and the relationship. In my case, that did not happen, perhaps because the bond was not strong enough in the first place. Maybe I wasn't able or willing to do what was necessary for it to endure the tough times.

At the end of the day, the answer to the "why" is a God question. My answer is simply that it just didn't work any more.

Heather's View

Both Dennis and I have been married previously. The divorce experience changed me as no other life experience has. I was broken open. Those difficult experiences taught both of us that relationships simply can't be taken for granted. Neither of us is comfortable with the terms "forever" or "always" any more. Regretfully, we are painfully aware that relationships don't always have happy endings, and we know relationships are fragile.

A happy marriage or long-term partnership doesn't just happen. It is created and re-created daily through the art of the little things which are really the big things. I make a choice daily to be married to Dennis and I value our partnership. I have both feet firmly planted in this relationship. We can speak words of love but isn't it powerful when we demonstrate our love through our daily actions? Love is not just a feeling; it is a verb, an *action* word.

When you buy a plant, you don't just stick it in the dirt and hope it grows. Your partnership is a precious plant that needs tending, care, conversation and renewal if it is to grow and withstand the pressures that aging, dwindling finances, time together and apart, failing health, adult children, aging parents, grandkids and changing identities can put on a relationship.

Good relationships must face challenge and resolve conflict. We certainly don't claim to have all the answers but I am grateful every day for a partner who is willing to look. We both use the expression "I am so lucky" as a statement of appreciation and, most days, we really mean it. On the days we don't, it's still a worthy goal, a statement of our intent and a positive affirmation. We are in this together, as a team!

Next Stage Challenges

In his book "The Joy of Retirement," professional counsellor David Borchard talks about some of the classic relationship challenges at this stage of life. See if you recognize yourself.

- We were attracted by our differences but there are a few traits I've always wanted to "modify" and now I can devote more time to the job of improving my partner!
- One of us places a strong value on social interaction and one of us treasures solitary time and solo endeavours. What will retirement together look like?
- He's ready to slow down and spend time together but I went back to work when the kids left. My career is just taking off.
- He/she has changed. I don't know this person any more and I don't know if I want to.
- She retired first and built a busy post-career life with her own friends and family and I'm just now retiring. I'm afraid of what a life together might look like.

Potential minefields indeed! You might not experience any of these scenarios but identifying your concerns and brainstorming ways to solve them would be a great place to start.

Recognizing a Prince or a Princess

Back when you were seeking a partner to share your life with, what were the non-negotiable qualities you looked for? What were the optional extras? Perhaps you have been together so long you no longer remember the list. I've kissed a frog or two in my life and if

I'm honest I must confess to a few frog-like behaviours of my own along the way. I despaired of ever finding a prince. Doing the homework for a course called Moving On required me to describe the qualities of a prince so I would recognize one when he came along. My prince would be *trustworthy*, *reliable* and *financially responsible*, *honest*, and an *engaged* and *willing partner*. Keen intelligence and a sense of humour would be nice too. I was past an age or stage in my life where hairline, waistline, wallet or his wardrobe were any more than superficial optional extras, way down my list. I learned to recognize basic, lasting core qualities, not the tall, dark and handsome fantasies of a younger age.

When Dennis and I had been dating for some time, I asked him why I hadn't met him sooner in my life. His answer flabbergasted me. "Heather, in the past you would never have seen a guy like me. You thought you were looking for something else." Many of us have trouble recognizing a *good* man or a *good* woman even when he or she is sitting on the other end of the couch! *Really* look at your partner right now and tell him or her five qualities you see and value. Write yourself a list in the Relationship section of Life Design and Planning.

That's A Lovely Carpet!

A young couple is waiting to see their minister for some pre-marriage counselling. He pokes his head in the room to tell them he will be a few more minutes and asks them both to look closely at the beautiful carpet on his office floor while they wait. As he joins them in the office, he asks each of them what they noticed about the carpet. The young woman commented on the richness of the colours and the beauty of the pattern. The future groom noticed the carpet's quality, deep pile and obvious value. "Did you see the flaw?" the minister inquired. Both indicated they had seen no flaw.

He showed them a small area in one corner of the carpet where the weaver had made an error in the pattern and the carpet was indeed flawed. He went on to tell them their partnership would be like the carpet. It was unlikely to be perfect but if they focused on the wonderful attributes that each of them possessed, that is what they would continue to see and appreciate about each other. If they focused instead on the flaws that too would affect their view and they would cease to see the beauty and richness in the relationship.

We all have flaws. If what we focus on grows, the opposite must also be true. What we don't focus on dies. Encouragement, support and appreciation develop our relationship. Unnoticed and unappreciated, our love and regard for each other dwindle.

I remember when one of my sons was small telling me he still cared about a cherished plush toy but that its *shine* had worn off. That's a risk in any longer-term relationship. We remain together but we allow the shine to wear off. How do we keep the shine?

Lots of Ways to Keep the Shine

In the aftermath of our respective marriage breakdowns, Dennis and I both volunteered for many years with an educational and support group called "Moving On" that was designed for people going through relationship breakdown and divorce.

Independently and together, we took many personal growth seminars and programs. In the course of that work, we met literally hundreds of wounded princes and princesses looking to heal their hearts and learn what it takes to thrive in their lives and in their relationships. We were also fortunate to meet many gifted teachers. With gratitude for all we learned from them, we share some of their teachings with you here.

Invest in Life Partnership

It's a Date

Our elderly neighbours have been married for over 60 years. Don still looks at Marnie with love and calls her "my bride" and Marnie fusses and refers to him as "my Donnie." We regularly see them dressed up and headed out for a *date*. They were Depression-era kids so their favourite night out is for dinner at Swiss Chalet. Marnie believes that their regular "date night" is a part of the glue that has kept them together for so long. Heck, who am I to argue with success?

Time Outs

In any close relationship, issues and conflicts arise. Defences are up and emotions are high, usually because we feel misunderstood and unfairly judged. In the worst cases, we are deeply hurt and offended. When this occurs, the first thing to consider is to take time out, not to sweep conflict under the rug where it will fester, but to take the time to settle down, gain some clarity, and reach beyond our instinctive response to lash out.

Heather and I differ in this regard since she usually prefers to deal with an issue or conflict immediately. I, on the other hand, usually require time and space. We have reached an agreement that when I request a time out, it will be no more than 24 hours and sometimes she counts the minutes!

Teach Yourselves How to Talk - Again

Now is the time to talk like you've never talked before and it's time to set up "the rules of engagement" for those conversations because some of them might be very emotionally charged.

Early on in our marriage, we took a weekend to attend a relationship workshop for couples. The two-day workshop was based on the book "Fighting for Your Marriage" by authors Howard J. Markman, Susan L. Blumberg, and Scott M. Stanley. The most important learning we took with us from that weekend (one which we are committed to using often in our relationship) is the Speaker-Listener Technique.

It is very important to discipline yourselves at the outset to deal with only one issue or conflict at a time. You will find it is counter-productive or destructive, in fact, to choose to pull everything out of your gunnysack all at once. It is also advisable to tackle the smaller issues first as a way to become familiar with and confident in using the technique.

The Speaker / Listener Technique

One person at a time has the floor (the speaker). The floor (the speaking time) is shared equally. "I" statements are used by the speaker, not "you" statements. Finger pointing and blame serve no purpose but to escalate the conflict, resolving nothing.

The other (the listener) does not speak but "listens" and is not thinking of what to say next or how to argue against the speaker. The listener is given time to paraphrase what s/he is hearing. "What I hear you saying is…" This step is essential to the process.

Check in with each other. If the listener is not "hearing" what the speaker is trying to say, the speaker tries again, and the listener paraphrases again. Keep this going for as long as necessary, taking turns where and when it makes sense to do so.

You may find it helpful to use an object that designates who has the floor, such as a small stone or a "talking stick" that you can hold in your hand. Whoever holds the object is the speaker. I tease Heather that I am going to carry a baseball bat to make it *very* clear when the floor is mine!

This technique is consistent with "seek *first* to understand, *then* to be understood" from Stephen Covey's "The Seven Habits of Highly Effective People" and it can work wonders. The first step to resolve conflict or accept differences is to acknowledge and respect the other's view. We don't need to *agree,* simply acknowledge and respect. To begin with, an intention to impose our view is a sure way of escalating conflict or of missing the opportunity to agree to disagree in harmony. One person's need to influence another has little chance without both feeling understood from the outset. Each of their truths is unarguable.

Behind Closed Doors

One of the really important conversations that middle-aged partners need to have *again* is one regarding their intimate life together. Yup, the S-E-X conversation. Sagging and less-than-limber bodies, changing hormone levels and self-image and a comfortable life in the rut of "the way it has always been" likely means we are overdue for a dialogue. The physical contact and emotional content of our intimate lives is too important to the health of our partnership to ignore. Our physical relationship is a primary means to express love and connection. Intimacy, In-To-Me-See. Intentional intimacy time can be sexual or non-sexual.

Linda and Charlie Bloom (bloomwork.com) were speakers at a couple's conference, which Dennis and I attended. They shared with us a frank view of the challenges and joys of middle-life sex. One of their suggestions was to develop a couple's shorthand we could use to communicate to our partner what we were up for. No pun intended.

Fast food, they said, is what you might expect – a quickie. Sometimes that's all either of you has the time, energy or interest for, *but* – a steady diet of fast food is not healthy for a loving partnership. Meat and potatoes is the regular old standby, routines and techniques you can both rely on. A meat and potatoes diet, while nourishing and comfortable, may be too routine and boring if the menu *never* changes. Gourmet dining, ah yes, that pulls out all the romantic stops! It might involve a special dinner, sharing a bubble bath, candle light, music and massage oil. Like a fabulous meal, it takes time and careful attention, and must be slowly savoured. It would be *much* too rich for a regular diet but what a special treat! Adventurous sex was the last option and allowed for anything *both* partners *mutually* agreed was acceptable but the idea was to get the creative juices flowing. Costumes anyone?

Grow Together

One of the commitments Dennis and I have on our respective life lists is a dedicated, formalized focus on our partnership at least once per year. Some years we attend a weekend event called "The Banff Couples Conference" (banffcouplesconference.com). This volunteer organization has been hosting couples conferences facilitated by trained counsellors and professionals for over 40 years now. In 2009, 86 couples attended the conference. An amazing energy is created when couples dedicated to the health of their partnership come together. To our knowledge, it is the only volunteer-run couples conference of this size in Canada. We highly recommend it!

In other years, we have taken couples courses or had special weekend getaways where the intention was on having conversations and planning for ways to improve our partnership that *didn't* involve the other person becoming who we wanted them to be. Each New Year's Eve we share a burning bowl ritual. We symbolically (and literally with words or symbols on paper) *burn* those aspects of the past year we *don't* want to take forward. We tell each other what we are grateful for and what we intend to take forward or to develop. Intimacy requires that you tell the truth about what is going on for you in the relationship. Common to all the couple's work we have done is an emphasis on communicating well, resolving conflict, having fun, and embracing the power of forgiveness.

Staying Current

A more regular relationship review to stay "current" with each other is a conversation style we learned from our friend Kerry Parsons at the Centre for Inspired Living. Using the speaker-listener technique, we give each other our celebrations, clearings and appreciations.

I'm currently celebrating my life and the lives of those I care about. I'm thrilled with your niece's engagement; I'm pleased I reconnected with an old friend; I celebrate my son's new job. Celebrations remind you both that there are *many* areas in your life worth celebrating.

Clearings create a place to have the difficult conversations. We develop intimacy in our partnership by revealing our hurts or situations where we felt unappreciated, overlooked or put down, *without blaming or judgment or character assassination.* This is an expression of *our* feelings. We aren't trying to tell our partner what they think or feel. To reduce the chances of slipping into or provoking anger, make this an "XYZ" statement. When you do X, in situation Y, I feel Z. When you walked away earlier while I was trying to tell you about my presentation, I felt (angry, irritated, frustrated, or sad). Our partner doesn't interrupt, respond, or provide any defence to this information until we have completed the third stage, our appreciation.

Appreciations are what you especially appreciate about your partner that you haven't shared with them today. None of us ever get tired of hearing we are appreciated. I appreciate that you picked up the items we needed at the store; I really appreciate that you make me a cappuccino each morning; thank you for noticing the special effort I made with dinner. Difficult conversations are easier to have when they are book-ended by the ways we celebrate and appreciate our lives together.

Appreciate Your Differences

We're different, not right and not wrong, just different. Often it was our differences that initially attracted us to our partners but those differences wear thin with the passing years. What might happen to our relationship if we could appreciate the differences and turn them into strengths? What if we saw the differences as something to cherish rather than a reason to criticize or if we recognized that there is more than one way to do *anything*? Are you making your differences separate you or bring you together? Honour what your partner knows. Know that you have the same goals but different ways of getting there. Nobody's perfect and this is not a shopping trip where we get to choose just *select* parts of the other. We can *accept* but we aren't required to *approve* of some of the things our partner is or does.

Dennis has many valuable traits that support me. He balances the chequebook and is meticulous with the laundry. He is organized. He always knows where everything is. These very traits make it difficult for him to accept that I can't seem to shovel the walk the *right* way or fold towels *correctly* and I accidentally leave things behind on airplanes. I could be bugged by my perception of his perfectionism or I can change my perception. I choose to concentrate on the tangible *gifts* his differences bring to me such as the magic, "self-filling" sock drawer, the cappuccino that appears each morning, and the gentle reminders to make the joint account deposit. When I thank him for his contribution and praise his *contribution* even as I may *expect* him to do his share around the house, he wants to do more.

We all operate that way. We can't be badgered, nagged or criticized into contributing but we can be appreciated into wanting to please each other. When we don't appreciate people, they go away, both physically and emotionally. What is the benefit to *you* of your different ways?

Who's in Charge?

One partner often feels they are *always* in charge of trip planning or social engagements as examples, and wants the other to step up to the plate and take action. It sounds fair, but who is really in charge?

A useful exercise that we picked up at a previous couples workshop has to do with clearly knowing who is in charge. Who is leading and who is following in any particular endeavour? This is always important for couples, but especially important for couples that are in the midst of life transition. Heather is quite comfortable leading. I will often say I'd rather not take the lead, but that is when the passive-aggressive side of me rears its head.

This is not necessarily a 50/50 deal yet it is important that the lead role is shared to some degree over time or there is an increasing risk of one person becoming resentful of always having the burden of responsibility, and the other of never being heard or having a voice. It is the leader's role, the one in charge at the time, to take responsibility and action in a fair and reasonable, mutually agreed timeframe. It is the follower's role to follow and to let go of any urge to control, even when it feels uncomfortable to do so.

Caution! This must not be about taking on a job, but having to do it the other's way. Give me a job, but only if you are willing to accept that it will be done *my* way.

So how do you know who is leading and who is following at any one time? You negotiate and reach agreement. There should be no grey areas, uncertainty, or miscommunication. The animated role-play exercise that we learned is easy, helpful and a little fun!

Imagine that you are both sitting in a rowboat. Move your arms as if you have oars and are actually rowing. It is probably best if both of you row in the same direction! The one who takes the lead remains silent but sets the rowing pace. The other says, "You are in charge and I am the best darn follower you've ever had." Some partners appear constitutionally unable to say this!

If you are to lead, you need to do that job. A key part of the leader's role is to keep the follower involved and informed. Do not attempt to throw the follower overboard, especially in rough water. If you are the follower and at some point find yourself trying to be in charge, get back in the boat and start rowing in sync with your leader. It is not a problem if for obvious reasons it makes sense to swap roles midstream. However, if an exchange of hats is decided upon, be sure to do the exercise again.

Invest in Life Partnership

Do Your Own Work

My friend Kerry, who has assisted hundreds of people in dealing with the aftermath of their separation and divorce in her Moving On program, tells me she is increasingly seeing mid-life people coming through her door. There is even a name for the phenomena: "grey divorce." She feels sad about this marked change in demographics because in her view; many of these people had imperfect partnerships that could likely have been salvaged had they received some attention before the love was lost.

Kerry's view is that people are looking *"out there"* for an avenue to contentment and happiness when that is really an *"inside job,"* requiring an introspective, soul-seeking, spiritual solution. We are all finding our way through this mid-life journey. Backed by psychologists and experience, her view shows that who we are and how we resolve differences shows up again in our next relationship. Changing your partner doesn't take us to the place of contentment we hope to find.

Changing ourselves by opening up or shifting our perceptions, clarifying our own life intentions and sharing with our partner who we *are* and, more importantly, who we are *becoming* leads us to greater life satisfaction.

I remember hearing a story about a woman who cut off both ends of the roast before putting the roast in the roasting pan. When asked why she did this, she simply answered that her mother and her grandmother had always done it that way. Curious, she decided to investigate and discovered a family tradition had been created because her grandmother's roasting pan was very small and she had to cut the ends off the roast to fit it in the pan.

How many of us have cut off pieces of ourselves in order to "fit in the pan?" Our task in mid-life is to discover the pieces we have cut off and become ourselves from the inside out. Those discoveries may well change you and thereby your relationship.

Define Your Relationship Expectations

Be clear that when *roles* change so do the *rules*. As we move into this next life stage, it is important to re-define our expectations of each other and re-examine our beliefs about what our relationship is now and what we wish it could be. It is tough to do when you are uncertain about your own identity.

Often in our partnership, our expectations are unspoken or for that matter unconscious. When they aren't met, we get angry and resentful. It's time to become aware and put them out in the open! You also need to be honest with your partner regarding your willingness to meet his or her expectations even if you don't share them.

I expect that we will both make contributions that enhance the quality of our relationship. I would like to define what that looks like. I expect that Dennis will support me in my personal growth. I expect that Dennis will contribute to the tasks necessary to operate our household and I'm happy to discuss and negotiate which tasks are to be blue jobs and which will be pink jobs. I'm in charge of pink and Dennis of blue. Not very evolved of us, is it? Our language may be sexist but there is gender equality. A blue job at our house is laundry and investment management is a pink job.

Of course, he has expectations too. The first task is to get clear and honest. The next task is to take a long hard look at whether those expectations are even reasonable. Is it reasonable to expect that even though you are both retired, one partner should continue to manage all the household operations? After many years together, do you expect that I *know* what you need or want without telling me? Is it reasonable to expect that you will spend *all* of your time together or for that matter, *all* of your time apart?

Go to Life Planning and Design (My Relationships) and complete the section "What are my relationship expectations going into retirement?" Consider your expectations of your partner with respect to issues such as family, finances, children, household chores, social interaction and friends, sex and fun.

One of my clients, an engineer, retired. His spouse was a homemaker. Homemaking spouses aren't as common as they once were. For the first few days, Bob sat at the kitchen table enjoying coffee and reading the paper, relaxing. After a couple of days, he looked at his wife and said, "Bette I've been watching the way you load the dishwasher. Your method is really very inefficient. You can get 50% more dishes in the dishwasher if you stack them differently." Bette just nodded patiently and said, "Thanks, Bob. I appreciate that." Things carried on until Bob mentioned, "Bette, when you vacuum, you make repeated passes over the same area of carpet. If you were to work from the outer perimeter into the center of the room in a grid pattern you could get your vacuuming done in half the time." It is no surprise that Bob is now in charge of dishwashers and vacuuming.

Retirement is a life stage where you should both be allowed to renegotiate the way things have always been. Have a discussion, or call it a negotiation. What life tasks or responsibilities do you wish were on your partner's list? In fairness, we have to look at the other side of the equation as well. What life tasks or responsibilities would you be willing to take over for your partner? Complete the Life Planning and Design exercise directed at Relationship - Life Partnership.

Maybe neither of you is willing to take on some jobs. Great! If nobody wants to mow the lawn, hire a lawn service or consider moving to a condo!

One of my clients suggested that it's healthier if couples don't retire at the same time. She felt her husband should retire first so he could learn how to operate all the household appliances and make some friends of his own! Consider the leisure and other activities you are looking forward to sharing with your partner, with friends and those you would prefer to pursue by yourself. What do you view as a group activity? Complete this list individually and then compare lists.

For Men Only

I first heard this when listening to a comedian on television. A man *really* needs to know only four words. Those words are: *Oh, ya, right... Sorry.* They can be spoken in almost any order (not leaving any out). Oh, sorry, ya... Right. Oh right, ya... Sorry.

My advice to all men in a significant relationship, retreads or not, is to say these four words often and with feeling. Your life may depend on it!

Keeping your sense of humour is so important. Heather and I regularly exchange a phrase we first learned from a bumper sticker: "I didn't say it was your fault. I said I was going to blame you."

And Finally

A healthy relationship is always a work in progress. We have vehicle inspections, regular physical exams and dental checkups. Our relationships surely deserve as much. I wonder what might be possible if you were to dedicate your energy to renew and revitalize your partnership. You could create a partnership where your partner accepts you as you are, seeks to know and understand you and wants you to be even more yourself. Now that's a life partner in the fullest, richest meaning of the term!

To do: Life Design and Planning
My Relationships (Life Partner)

Relationship

Friendships

What is a friend ... *a single soul dwelling in two bodies.*

Aristotle

Who is a friend? A friend is someone who knows all about you, likes you, and has no immediate plans for your improvement.

Friendships

Over a lifetime, friends will come and go but some precious ones will stay. Author Art Linkletter calls our spouse our life partner, and our long-term friends, "light partners." Friendships run their course; friends move away, and friends pass away. Heather's mother, at 92 years old, says she has few friends left because she has outlived them all. The key for her will be to keep making younger friends.

When you think back through your friendship history how many former schoolmates from elementary or even high school do you regularly keep in touch with? Are you still in touch with university roommates? What about former team-mates, parents of your kids' friends, or work associates from your last job? Throughout much of our life, new relationships have come into our world without too much effort on our part. They have come through school, our children, our work and outside associations. It seems we were always meeting new people. Now, our relationship-building skills are probably a bit rusty.

It's an Evolution

As we move into our next life phase, creating new friendships requires both an intention and some social skills. We may need to look further afield and make a greater effort to build our social capital. Former work colleagues may or may not have a part to play in our new life. If they are still working, they may not have time to maintain the association and perhaps you will cease to have much in common. The glue may be gone from those relationships or they may not have the qualities needed to sustain a lasting friendship. Perhaps you will choose some new role models or mentors that help you to adapt to your new identity. None of us remains the same.

Even our old friendships must evolve if they are to retain their significance, which is an important aspect of friendship to come to grips with. It is a real pitfall when retiring to underestimate or to discount the effect on our well-being of losing friends and having less social interaction. If some of our need in this regard is being met through our work, the question we must ponder is how that need will be met once we retire. I am not trying to alarm anyone here, because this is by no means a dead end. On the contrary, the risk is that of being unaware and being blindsided after the fact.

I regularly meet for lunch with a few of my "hand-picked" former work colleagues. This began as a conscious choice when I retired and, over several years, these friendships have needed to change because the work life and personal life parameters have changed. I value these part-time lunch friends because the relationships help me to meld my past with the present in a manner that is meaningful and healthy. In their case, I believe I am also helping to give them glimpses into their future. I hope I am a good role model for a future they can look forward to.

Taking Inventory

Don't take this friendship question lightly; it's time to take an inventory. In Life Planning and Design under Relationships you'll find a large square with "ME" in the center. The ME is you. Write the names or initials of "others" in your life in relation to their connection with you. Most will place their life partner close to ME, and their children a little further out, with siblings, other family members and friends fanning out from there. Closer friends would be shown closer on the diagram than occasional social contacts. Who knows you well? How solid is your social network? If you are an extrovert, the inventory may reveal a large cast of characters. If you are an introvert, it may include just a few well-chosen friends. Chances are if you are female, your social network is larger than your male counterpart's.

Several of my male clients felt lost when they first retired. They left most of their male companionship back at the office and were surprised when their partner or spouse had a busy social calendar that didn't include them. It's healthy for each partner to have their own social contacts – yours, mine and ours. It's unrealistic and unhealthy to expect that *any* one person has the capacity to meet *all* of our relationship needs.

In their book "What Color is Your Parachute – For Retirement?" Richard Bolles and John Nelson describe three levels or types of relationship.

Pleasant relationships are based on your *interests* – your golf buddies, hiking group, fellow book club member. We have fun and we share enjoyment and experiences with these folks. In retirement, we can build this source of potential new friends by joining new groups or organizations that connect with our personal interests such as running clubs, quilting groups, art classes, or gyms.

Engaging relationships are based on our *strengths* or our *skills*. In these associations, we are challenged and slip into a shared sense of *flow*. That might mean working jointly on a budget for the church or a membership drive for a volunteer organization. New friends can be found wherever our skills and talents for organizing, planning, building, and creating would be needed and valued.

Meaningful relationships, according to Bolles and Nelson, are based on *values* and we share a sense of purpose with these people. Volunteer organizations, religious or spiritual communities, couples groups will all bring us into contact with others that share our values.

Key relationships likely include some of each of these elements and, according to the authors, would produce a more lasting relationship, but it certainly isn't necessary for us to relate on all three levels to enjoy another's company. I think it is useful to look at our social network or community and consider whether we do have some relationships where we have fun, and feel challenged and deeply connected.

Dennis and I have created our own "club." It started some years ago as a grown-up birthday party for Dennis, who had never had a party as a child, but it has become our way to cherry-pick a community filled with people we love who didn't know one another. We felt that all our great friends should meet.

We also enjoy travelling and hiking with friends. We are both directionally challenged, so friends not only provide wonderful companionship, but provide us with the directions home.

A self-titled *dis*organization set up strictly for fun is the Red Hat Society; you may know them through their wardrobe statement of a red hat and a purple dress. Sorry gents, this one is just for sassy spirited women 50 and over. Their only objective is fun. Check the web for local groups or start one in your area (redhatsociety.com).

Of course, friendship is a two-way street. To *have* a good friend we must *be* a good friend. What qualities do you bring to your friendships and what qualities are you looking for? Do they include trust, reciprocity, respect and support, and room to be authentic? Do we show our assets and our flaws? Do we want intellectual stimulation or shared interests? Do we offer a positive outlook, reliability, open-heartedness, fun and open-mindedness?

Resolving Conflict

We would add an important ability, which is to face and deal with conflict. In the recent past, Heather and I had two long-term friendships end. The reason became clear to us once the emotional dust had settled, and it had to do with conflict. In all close and meaningful friendships, conflicts will arise from time to time. The seriousness or level of conflict will vary, but issues will always arise. As long as the values of integrity, honesty, and trust are maintained in a friendship, conflict represents an opportunity to strengthen the friendship.

When a conflict arises, if neither party is prepared to deal with it without being defensive and attached to being right, then the friendship will be damaged and may end. Fragile one-sided friendships are not the kind of friendships to hang our hat on.

Stand by Me

Art Linkletter and Mark Victor Hansen describe their view of the important functions our mid- and later-life friendships serve in their book "How to Make the Rest of Your Life the Best of Your Life".

Support during hard times
Motivation to reach goals or try new things
Exposure to new ideas
A positive competitive influence
Nurturing
Improve our mood
Sharing humour
Spur us to access health care or take better care of ourselves

Not having friends may be hazardous to your health! The MacArthur Study of Successful Aging concluded that people with strong social connections enjoy better health. Other studies have suggested they also lead to a longer life. Extend your life and improve your health – make a friend. Friends of the four-legged variety also count!

Ensure your friends span the generations. We learn from our young friends how to text message and use FaceBook, and from our 90+ year old neighbours who talk about their long life experience.

Heather and I have a list of friends with whom we want to grow old. These friends are a chosen family. For us, particularly as we age, our relationship with our close friends is a life cornerstone. Being conscious of this, we are committed to keep in touch and spend time with these people on a regular basis. Everyone's lives are so busy even when retired that only by making this a stated intention and following through with commitments on the calendar will these friendships stand the test of time. What relationships do you need to direct more energy to? Where and how do you plan to extend your friendship circle?

To do: Life Design and Planning
            My Relationships (Friends, Family and Friends)

Relationship

Parenting

> *Parents are the bones on which*
> *children cut their teeth.*

Peter Ustinov

Parenting

Our relationships with our children, stepchildren, and grandchildren are significant for so many of us. Parenting is a job that never ends. We can't retire from it and it is such a major aspect of our lives we must acknowledge that and include it when we are planning for retirement.

At midlife, few of us are dealing with young children; they are emerging or independent adults. The very concept of an adult child seems an oxymoron. In past generations, you were either a child *or* an adult. On a day variously defined by age, duties or cultural expectations, you crossed an invisible line and were treated differently and held to different expectations at home and in society.

Now, higher costs in living independently, increased education requirements and schooling costs all act as a barrier to early independence. Add to that the creature comforts that life at home provides and all the factors conspire to give our emerging adults a slower start. Even when they do leave the family home, many will still need financial and certainly emotional assistance from us. In many families and cultures, this extended home stay is encouraged and expected. In other households, the nudge to leave the nest is stronger, particularly if you feel their slow start is infringing on your freedom, and your own family placed a high value on early independence. Many parents are impatient to reclaim control of their own time, living space and finances without the myriad obligations and weight of responsibility that naturally come with the parenting package.

Things begin to change on the home front as we exert some adult expectations on our children to do more for themselves and around our home, and as they make more independent choices and decisions. When they are at our home or return home, we need to establish, together, the terms of their stay.

A Delicate Dance

As the parents of young children, we danced a delicate dance between rushing forward to support them as they took those first tentative steps and stepping back to let them experience the joy and the challenge of personal accomplishment. As they grew, we stepped back a little more with each passing year. For most of us, the ultimate goal is to take our hands off the reins entirely, while nurturing our connection and remaining supportive and willing to advise or offer opinions, *when asked.*

In my own experience and that of many of my female clients and friends, that goal was more easily expressed than accomplished. Few of us could deal with our *own* feelings of anxiety and discomfort while watching them struggle with an issue, so we stepped in and robbed them of opportunities to demonstrate their capabilities. Of course, as they aged, it appeared to us that the stakes got higher. The problems we were trying to protect them from were no longer a scraped knee but drugs and gangs, drinking and poor choices. From their side of the fence, it looked as though we didn't trust their judgment or support their decisions. We told ourselves we just wanted to keep them safe and save them from mistakes.

How is it we find it so easy to give them credit for their accomplishments but *we* take on the responsibility for their mistakes? Naturally, these newly adult children and fully independent adult children will make mistakes and life choices that will disappoint us. *Both sides,* parent and child, likely fall short of our highest expectations of each other.

It's Your Life Now

Our friend Gordon described a discussion with his mother when he was a young adult studying to become a psychologist. He hoped to begin a dialogue about how her parenting had affected him growing up. Her reaction to the conversation was to tell him, "Fiddlesticks! I did the best I could. It's *your* life now!"

Depending on their age, *it is* their life now. Our adult children bear the responsibility for making their *own* lives work. We are caring observers, available and open. Sometimes we can smooth their path and provide an ear. We can commiserate or cheer them on but we can't change them or take responsibility for their success or their failure. Our role is to create a relationship with who they *are* and insist they begin to see us as *we* are, human and fallible, with needs of our own.

Author Dr. Ruth Nemzoff describes this stepping back as *second-stage parenting.* She disagrees with conventional advice that suggests we "let go" and bite our tongue in our relationships with our adult children. Her view is that we let go only of our expectations of who we wanted them to be and that we develop our ability to communicate with them so we don't have to bite our tongue. This involves walking a line between intimacy and independence, nurturing and autonomy. Second-stage parenting, she points out, will last many more years than the first stage did!

It's important that we move to a more equal relationship and an adult style of communicating without offending or shutting down the adult child. Sometimes it seems that they question everything we believe to be true. We can't make pronouncements or withdraw into judgmental silence if we don't share their viewpoint but want to retain and strengthen our bond. There are unexpected rewards in expanding our own life view. We can ask questions and offer opinions, letting them know that ours is just one voice of many and it may be out of date. It is acceptable to give advice; just don't *expect* it will be followed!

Step-Parenting

For a lot of us, step-parenting is a role we took on as a result of choosing a relationship with someone who already has children. Had anyone told me early on that step-parenting would be one of the single most challenging aspects of my second marriage, I'm not sure I would have believed them, nor would I have understood.

Heather and I have an expression that we often use with one another when we notice that a step-kid issue is beginning to drive a wedge between us. One says to the other, *"Your kids are worse than mine."* Of course, neither of us takes that statement literally, but it serves to send a signal that it's time to take a step back to avoid damaging our relationship. We tend to get very protective and positional when it comes to our *own* children as opposed to our step-children.

There is an unquestionable relationship difference, for me, between a child of my own and a step-child. The emotional connection is not the same. Perhaps this would be less true if I became a step-parent of a young child or baby and especially if the birth mother or father whose role I was to step into was absent. Undoubtedly, there are major adjustments for the step-child too but I cannot speak for a step-child. I really have no idea what it might be like for them. I never had a step-parent.

Until I had a child, I would not have taken a bullet for anyone. Once I became a father, my life changed forever. When I glance back at that moment, I realize that in an instant I was no longer the most important person in the world. There was now a life I considered more valuable to me than my own, that of my newborn child.

This depth of emotional tie does not usually exist with a step-child. A close relationship with step-children is certainly possible and desirable, but the natural connection is simply not the same. However, caring about a child (adult children included) with a little emotional distance can sometimes allow for better parenting decisions. You know the tough love stuff can be very difficult for the child's parent because their own discomfort gets in the way of their choices. The parent's emotional tie to the child is a big deal. In fact, it is sometimes such a big deal that s/he can't see the forest for the trees when trying to set boundaries and limitations, and follow through with consequences. Tying the parent and step-parent roles together can create some well-balanced parenting decisions.

My daughter, who happens to be the oldest of our four children, jokes with the family by saying, "I am the favourite child." She claims this role because, as she happily points out, she combines financial independence, a physically active lifestyle and she lives away from home. We joke back that should she be the one to produce our first grandchild, she will *definitely* win the award!

Heather and I have grandchildren on our life lists but, of course, we aren't in charge of that! If that hope becomes reality, I wonder whether there will be a difference between being a grandparent versus a step-grandparent. I don't think so but only time will tell. We look forward to welcoming grandchildren.

A Work In Progress

Our relationships are always a work in progress. Ask your adult children, step-children, and daughter-in-law or son-in-law what they expect from you along the way and examine your expectations of them. We all have personal, societal and cultural expectations regarding the role of "doting" grandmother, or "dutiful" daughter-in-law and "well-behaved" children.

Part of being an adult is understanding another's point of view and presenting our own honestly and openly. We all deserve to be heard. It is easier to keep trying, however, when we aren't keeping score. Recognize that good relationships aren't always smooth and adult relationships must be mutual. Ask, listen, talk and repeat as needed!

We all know parenting doesn't end when our child becomes an adult. The parenting relationship, like no other, is "for better or for worse, until death do us part." Even if they move away and contact is limited, it remains a relationship for life.

Invest in Parenting

Each stage of the parenting journey demands that we grow, accommodate, drop judgment and adjust expectations to come through tough times. The evolution continues for life, through first-stage parenting that saw them grow from babies to reach their emerging adult selves, to second stage parenting and their launch from the nest into independence. This brings with it the growing pains of negotiating an equal relationship where everyone's needs and interests are appreciated.

Next comes accepting their relationship choices and possibly negotiating a way through weddings or other lifestyle choices that may test our tolerance. Their life partners bring other personalities and another set of expectations, new primary loyalties and new in-laws into both your lives. You may be called on to accept life choices that cause both you and your adult child pain. Once again, we change and grow, learn, and love.

Grandchildren may (or may not) arrive along with your notions *and* your adult child's on how these children should be raised and what your role as grandparent should be. Eventually, life comes full circle and we may need to accept our children's role as our caretakers, monitoring our choices, supporting but not controlling, accepting and not judging and so on and on it goes.

To do: Life Design and Planning
             My Relationships (Family and Friends, Adult Children)

Relationship

Three Generations

Every generation needs a new revolution.

Thomas Jefferson

Three Generations

History tells us that every generation claims to be wiser than the one that came before!

Let me begin by saying, "If your life doesn't fit the picture painted here, that's great. You are among the fortunate few! You may still find it interesting and entertaining, so keep reading because it's short.

Those of us who were born in the 1950s are commonly referred to as the "Sandwich Generation." If you are reading this book, I'll take the liberty of assuming that you are most likely one of "us." I don't appreciate being labelled or categorized but in this case there are some aspects of the label and the category that ring true. In fact, sometimes it feels to me as though we are a chopped liver or even a baloney sandwich!

Sandwich refers to the fact that many of us find ourselves caught in the middle between dependent aging parents and dependent adult children. In 2006, Statistics Canada reported that about 25% of

Canadians between the ages of 45 to 64 provide some level of care to older family members. Of those, 77 % are also working. Another Stats Canada study determined that as high as 60 % of Canadians ages 20 to 24 still live at home with their parents. That sandwich covers a lot of us! Add in the many variations on this theme such as blended families, adult children returning to the nest with children in tow or pursuing further education, parents still on their own but needing additional support, and parents in extended care facilities and most of us are affected in some way!

There is no one-size-fits-all family. If you happen to be an only child and a single parent as well, you have one of the most demanding and challenging relationship roles of all. Somewhere please find the time to make *you* a first priority. You undoubtedly need and deserve it!

Sandwich Assistance

Some of us have developed a pattern of believing that we need to do *everything* ourselves. We don't recognize that we could use help so we don't look for it and we aren't great at accepting it when it's offered. There are resources available to support us but we need to take the time and make the effort to search those out, find what suits our situation, and utilize them.

A good place to start is a new Government of Canada guide called Services for Seniors. The guide is designed for Canadians 50 and over who are planning their retirement, and for the families of seniors or their caregivers.

You can view or download the guide at servicecanada.gc.ca or call 1-800-O-Canada or e-mail guide@canada.gc.ca.

Author Patty Randall has written a Canadian guidebook titled "Let's Talk – The Care Years: Taking Care of Our Parents, Planning for Ourselves." You can visit her website at (longtermcare-canada.com). Patty writes about the help that we and our aging parents will require when we reach the *care years*, or the "end of our biological warranty period." She describes two key roles – a *care-manager* and the *hands-on caregiver* and the important decisions each will make.

Elderwise (elderwise.ca) gives information and support for the sandwich generation through publications such as their free newsletter.

Impact on Retirement Planning

So what does this have to do with Retirement Rocks and launching your retirement, you ask? On the surface, perhaps nothing but if we dig a little deeper it has a whole lot to do with it. Let's look briefly at three generations; our parents as generation #3, those of our vintage, generation #2, and our children as generation #1. Why on earth did I give our children the #1 billing? Do you really need to ask?

Our parents regularly worked to an older age than we will prior to retiring. Their parents had often passed away by the time they retired. Most of us desperately wanted our independence as soon as we could possibly get it. By the time our parents retired, we were largely independent and had left home. I know I did. It was the only way to get my own room!

How does that scenario fit today? We want to retire sooner, our parents are living longer, and our children generally do not become independent (out of the house and self-sufficient financially) until a much later age and stage. Heather and I refer to it as being launched and off the payroll. Of our four children, two are mostly launched and two are not. In my moments of intolerance and frustration, you'll hear me describing the two at home as roommates that don't pull their weight! Don't get me wrong. They are fine individuals and we will continue to do what we can for as long as it takes to get them launched.

The circumstance we, and others, are caught in affects our retirement plans. Financially, there are ongoing obligations and necessities for both dependent parents and adult children. Our living costs may be higher than we like, we may need to put off our plans to downsize, to relocate or even to travel very often. Even if Heather and I did not have kids at home, we wouldn't go far as long as Heather's mother needed us.

Isn't it interesting that most of us still refer to our adult children as *kids*? I was financially independent and had left home by the time I was 20. Heather's story is similar. Heck, she went away to university primarily to escape the midnight curfew her mother staunchly upheld. "What is a curfew?" asks generation #1. Wait a minute! This is beginning to sound like the type of story where my son asks, "Dad, is this one of those 'I went up hill both ways to school' stories?"

Are we there yet? In many instances, the freedom we hopeful retirees are anticipating, from both a financial and a lifestyle perspective, just isn't there yet. Be patient; it is coming. We need to make sure that this situation does not stop us in our tracks. We must stay the course, focus on our retirement intention, and determine feasible interim steps wherever possible.

Generational Views of Money

I find it interesting how views regarding money differ from one generation to the next. Our parent's generation felt responsible for their role as *custodian* of the family fortune. Most of them have, or had, a very difficult time spending their hard-earned money on themselves. Many of them designed their wills to enable them to continue to manage the family fortune from the grave.

I had a cherished great aunt who was stricken with Parkinson's disease. She eventually became almost completely physically dependent. She was in a shared room in an extended-care facility and she had been given a fancy new bed to use for a two-week trial. With just the push of a button, she could move this bed in any direction she wanted in order to make it easy for her to get in and out and to be more comfortable. She loved it. I asked her if she was going to keep it. She said, "It costs $2,000. I can't possibly." She had close to a half a million dollars in the bank. She had no children and she was 85 at the time. When she passed away at 87, she left most of her money to her 22 nieces, nephews, and grand nieces and nephews. Bless her heart. That's commonly generation #3's view of money.

Generation #1's view of money is usually quite the opposite. They would much rather spend generation #2's money than their own if they can and often we give them that option and opportunity. No wonder they want to remain "kids!"

Commonly, generation #2 has worked hard, saved poorly, and invested heartily in the future of generation #1. We are hopeful that our bank of Mom or Dad job is near completion and we won't have any trouble relinquishing that role of custodian for the future generations. Many of us will try to help generation #1 with their first house or condo purchase, and/or generation #0 with their education if and when we are in a position to do so. It won't feel like necessity or obligation by then will it?

In Conclusion

If you are a member of generation #1 and are offended by what I have to say about the three generations, I will be sure to read your rebuttal or opposing point of view in *your* book. Actually, come to think of it, what are you doing reading this book anyway?

I have a confession to make. Our elderly neighbours call Heather and I "you kids" and we *really* like it. "How are you kids?" they will ask. Heck, given a choice I would stay a kid as long as possible too!

If you are a part of the *sandwich generation*, don't lose heart. Regretfully, the old guard *will* pass and thankfully, the new guard will take up the torch. Your role is to prepare, as best you can, for your own time in the sun.

To do: Life Design and Planning
My Relationships (Adult Children, Parents and In-laws)

Finances

Money is intended to be of service to us, not the other way around. Thank you, Dad, for that life lesson.

How Much is Enough
Net Worth Statement
Cash Flow Statement
Company Pensions
Government Benefits
Personal Savings and Investments
Tax Strategies in Retirement
Estate Planning and Life Insurance

LIFESTYLE | RELATIONSHIP | FINANCES

Finances

How Much is Enough?

Discontent makes rich men poor.
Content makes poor men rich.

Benjamin Franklin

How Much Is Enough?

Ask any roomful of people considering retirement, "Who worries whether or not they have enough money?" Virtually everyone in the room will raise their hand, particularly following setbacks in real estate and stock market investments.

The interesting thing about the concept of "enough" is that we all measure it differently. Let me assure you that your level of income has *very little* to do with your sense of abundance, sufficiency or "enough." One of the many lessons that I learned from my clients is that each of us has a different notion of what abundance is and all of us are right!

One of my favourite clients had one of the most abundant lives I ever had the privilege to witness, and she was living this abundant life on a $2,000 per month disability income. She had two things she described as her "blessed indulgences" – good red wine and expensive bubble bath. Now on $2,000 a month in an expensive city like Calgary, she couldn't drink a LOT of good wine, but when she opened a bottle she truly savoured *every* drop, often while soaking in the bathtub. I used to tease her that, given what she paid for her bubble bath, she should be drinking the bathwater and bathing in the wine!

I also worked with a surgeon. He and his spouse simply could not get by on annual earnings of $700,000. To this couple, the big house, new cars, fabulous vacations, great furnishings and wardrobes were "essentials." There was never going to be "enough" even if they won a large lottery or received a big inheritance. They lived their lives from a viewpoint of scarcity.

It is important to define what constitutes *enough* or what abundance is for *us*. Some of us will think of it in terms of dollars per month or per year. "Enough money is $60,000 per year, or enough money is $4,000 per month." Some of us will think in terms of a percentage of our pre-retirement income – maybe 50%, 60% or 70%. Many of us won't be able to come up with our own number. I can't tell you how many times clients made statements such as "Tell me what the *average* Canadian needs" or "What do *most* of your other clients require?"

In the back of our minds, each of us operates on some tangible and intangible measures about what is "enough." These "enough" measures are certainly different for someone living in poverty in a third-world country than they are for the average North American. Furthermore, there is no "average" North American!

If we decide to have pasta for dinner, some of us will lovingly make our own sauce, some will go out and buy an inexpensive jar of prepared sauce, and some will say "Who cooks?" and go out to a high-end Italian restaurant for a pasta dinner. Chances are that each of us would describe ourselves as average.

Tell me what your life experience *feels* like when you have enough, and I can help you measure what it will take to reach your "enough" goal. This attitude of "what is enough" is more a sense of what brings *felt* abundance into your life. Abundance doesn't necessarily mean diamonds and big fancy houses. Most of us don't live the lifestyle of the rich and famous now and don't aspire to live that way in retirement.

To explain what the heck I'm talking about, I'll tell you some of my "enough" measures. I know I have enough if I can afford a cleaning person. I don't care if I'm living in a tent but I don't want to be the one to sweep and clean and neither does Dennis. I love to entertain at home. Enough allows me to continue entertaining friends and family without having to think too long and hard about the cost of doing so. I should also add that I'm *adaptable*, and we *all* are. For example, I don't need to serve guests filet mignon. I want the pleasure of their company and I know they will be happy with hamburgers.

Enough Measures

Here are some thoughts from clients and attendees at our retirement seminars. Enough is:

- Not changing my present standard of living
- Maintaining a second home or a recreation property
- Assisting my kids with their education or helping them with the down payment on their first home
- Helping my daughter pay for her wedding
- Buying a new car every four years

- Taking a "big" trip to an exotic location every two or three years in retirement
- Taking several weekend "getaways" every year
- Golfing three times per week
- Helping my grandchildren with their education
- Leaving an inheritance to my children of $X each

Go to "My How Much is Enough Measures" (Life Design and Planning) and jot down your enough list. Don't share your list with a partner until you both have completed it. Go back to each item and see if you can estimate a cost for it in "today's" dollars. How much of a down payment do you want to help each child with? How big and expensive a wedding?

Dennis and I define our trips in terms of "big," "moderate" and "little" trips. For us, big trips don't require a five-star hotel or expensive restaurants, but we aren't willing to rough it any more. "Big" trips can cost up to $10,000 per person after factoring in airfare, accommodation, meals, and so on. We may not be able to have a big trip every year but our "enough" measure is a plan for every other year for five or six trips to places that are top priorities on our "Life List." We have also defined "little" trips and "moderate" trips and included those in our plan. For a little trip, we stay in a tent or an Alpine Club of Canada hut and do some hiking for a weekend. A moderate trip might be to escape Canada's winter for a couple of weeks at a sun spot, or travel to visit friends in other parts of Canada.

What about the flipside of abundance? What is scarcity to you? Lynne Twist in her book, "The Soul of Money" identifies what she describes as the three lies of scarcity: (1) there is never enough, (2) more is better, and (3) that's just the way it is.

Many of us put the "don't have enough" roadblock in the way of our retirement plans and continue working without consideration of the possible alternatives. Having "enough" looms so large we don't look for alternatives or imagine another way to live. Part of this is defining what is truly most important to us – retiring sooner or growing the pot bigger? When we do finally take the plunge and step away from our primary career and into our next life stage, most of us stop worrying about the money and scale back in the ways necessary to live within our means.

Think back to your early days starting out on your own. What did your bookcase look like? Was it bricks and boards, concrete blocks, milk cartons? What did your first couch look like? How many bathrooms were in the home you grew up in? How many cars were in your driveway?

You may not choose to go back to living that way but were you unhappy or dissatisfied? What if you couldn't have a trip every year? Would you settle for a trip every other year or every third year, or could you become an "armchair" traveller and still enjoy your life? What if you couldn't replace the car when you wanted to? Would you simply replace it when you could?

We are all very adaptable. Most of us will change our spending and consuming behaviour to suit our present circumstance and we already have *concrete life experience* of doing so in the past. Many will spend too much time wanting *more* and too little time planning how they might experience a rich and juicy life with *enough*.

Many women share a secret concern about being a bag lady. The term "bag lady" is exclusive to females. When you're a "bag man" that's really kind of glamorous because you carry money for the

Mafia. Male terms for "not enough" such as hobo or tramp carry a degree of romanticism!

Bag Ladies

One of my clients decided to collect stories from her girlfriends. Her question was "If your life was reduced to a shopping cart, which one item would you put in the cart?" How is that for bringing your life down to the essentials? One girlfriend would have a Baccarat crystal wine goblet. Her thought was "If I'm reduced to drinking cheap booze, I'm going to drink it in style." Another friend said she would carry her sewing machine in the cart. She would make her way hemming pants or stitching up shirts and could trade those services for other goods. Clever, yes?

My favourite was the gal who would have nothing but a long black tube of jersey knit fabric. She would roll it up as a skirt to wear with a tidy white blouse and march right in to funeral lunches for tea and sandwiches, leading everyone to assume she knew the deceased. In the evening, she would tuck it up under her armpits as an evening gown and march into wedding receptions as dinner was served!

What brilliant examples of adaptability.

One of the exercises I ask seminar attendees to complete is to describe to me what they would *still have* if they lost *all* of their possessions. They answered – the support of their partner, the love of their children, their health, and their ability to earn a living. What else?

Now revisit your "enough" list. Spend some serious front-end time thinking about the "enough" measures in your life.

Measuring Enough

Let's look at some concrete ways to measure "enough" financially.

#1 How much is enough to retire on?

For a "back of the envelope" or ballpark number, use the rule of thumb given by Dr. Sherry Cooper in her book, "The New Retirement." She maintains that we need a nest egg of 20 times what we spend each year in pre-tax income in order to die broke. If we want to leave an estate behind, we will need 25 times that amount. For example, if we spend $50,000 pre-tax per year and have *no* company *or* government benefits, the required "pot" is $1,000,000.

Many Canadians will receive both CPP and OAS (see chapter on Government benefits for details). At maximum, for 2009, CPP is approximately $10,000 per year at age 65. OAS at maximum benefit with no claw-back will add about $6,200 per year. The $50,000 per year could be reduced by just over $16,200 if we retire at age 65. Our nest egg requirement becomes 20 x $33,800 or $676,000. You would also deduct company pension benefits and any other retirement income you will receive from the income requirement and thereby reduce the required nest egg. Note these are pre-tax numbers and most of us think of our spending requirements in after-tax dollars.

Dr. Cooper, quoting numerous sources to support her estimate, has assumed a 5% average annual return on the portfolio *after* adjusting for inflation of 3% and a 30-year retirement period. She goes on to point out that history suggests the portfolio asset mix would need to be 50% or better in equities (stocks) with the balance in bonds. The withdrawal rate or drawdown from the portfolio would begin at 4%

in your first year of retirement and rise by a 3% inflation rate each year thereafter. If you anticipate a longer retirement, the nest egg would need to be larger.

Put pencil to paper using the How Much is Enough Forecaster and Future Value Tables located in Life Design and Planning and in the Financial Appendix to calculate the future value of your own nest egg based on your current balances, savings rates and expected rates of return. The most important factor to focus on is your spending. We'll do that in the chapter on cash flow.

#2 Another Look at How Much?

Financial calculators are very useful tools. Chances are, if you are an accountant, an IT type or an engineer, you've already created your own spreadsheets or forecasting models. For those who haven't created their own, there are many available for you to use. The challenge with many of them is that we are required to make assumptions with regard to rate of return, inflation and other factors and we may feel ill equipped to "guesstimate."

Have a look at several different sites and forecast programs. If you are not required to enter your own assumptions, be sure you understand the assumptions built into the program.

www.fidelity.ca/take the challenge
www.seclonlogic.com
www.taxtips.ca
www.retirementrocks.ca
www.dinkytown.com   Note this is an American site; use the
                        "Canadian Calculators" tab.

Most of the major Canadian banks and financial services firms have free online calculators available. If you are participating in a group RRSP or pension program at work, chances are your company or the financial services supplier provides forecasting programs.

#3 Consult an Advisor

Working with your own advisor, hiring a fee-for-service financial planner or visiting the investment people at the institution where you normally bank are all options to help you get a grasp of the required nest egg.

With any of these options, we start to develop an awareness of where we stand and where we need to develop discipline and focus in our savings and investments. If there is a serious gap between what you feel you need as retirement income and what your present resources can provide, it's time to consider alternatives.

Are we going to work longer or perhaps work part-time throughout our early retirement? Part-time work to delay or reduce the drawdown of our retirement resources will be a key part of the solution for many of us.

Can we take another look at our anticipated expenses? Are we willing to change some spending decisions *now* for earlier financial freedom? Bag lunches and forgoing the morning latte are easier when we know what we're working toward. Is the retirement goal important enough that we'll choose to put off buying a new car or going on an expensive holiday?

Is it possible to earn a higher return on our investments? Think long and hard about this one! It's the "easiest" option to call your financial advisor and say, "I need you to get a 12% or 15% return on all my investments." Is it even possible and would you tolerate the higher risk of such a portfolio? Are you prepared to sell personal assets or downsize the home in order to take some money off the table? Maybe that second car isn't needed. The CAA estimates that the expense of operating a vehicle is over $12,000 a year including depreciation. Perhaps those funds could be better utilized.

One of the factors in the calculation is life expectancy. Actuarial tables for 2006 show life expectancy of 83.7 years for women and 76.9 years for men. Studies have shown if a woman reaches age 65, there is a 53% chance she will reach age 85, and a 31% chance she will reach age 90. A man of 65 has a 36% chance of reaching age 85, and a 17% chance of reaching age 90. I've had clients say, "Well I'm not likely to live past 82." I would smile and ask them what their "plan B" was!

We will look next at Net Worth and Cash Flow statements. Both of these are vital to creating the retirement nest egg.

To do: Life Design and Planning
          My Finances - How Much is Enough Measures
          My Finances - How Much is Enough Forecaster

A How Much is Enough Forecaster worksheet and calculator are available from our web site (www.retirementrocks.ca).

Finances

Net Worth Statement

*Your net worth is what remains after bad
habits are subtracted from good ones.*

Benjamin Franklin

Net Worth Statement

Three Fundamental Questions

When you visit a financial planner or you create your own financial
forecast, there are three questions to ask:

1. When do you wish to stop work? There has to be a "plan
   to" date even if we don't hold you to it.

2. How big is the retirement pot you have to work with now?
   To answer question number two we need to prepare a Net
   Worth Statement; that's the subject of this chapter.

3. How much do you spend? This is frankly *the* most important
   question. How much we spend has the single largest
   influence on the size of the pot we will need for retirement.
   We'll cover that in the chapter on Cash Flow.

A Net Worth Statement takes into account everything *owned* less everything *owed*. It describes our ASSETS minus our LIABILITIES. The remainder is our NET WORTH. If we were examining a company, that number or value would represent Shareholder's Equity.

Your Net Worth Statement should be viewed as your financial report card and, like a report card, it points out where you are doing well and where you have some work to do.

Sample Framework for Net Worth Statement

	OWN	(A)	OWE	(B)
	Asset	$ value	Liability	$ amount
1	Cash savings		CC debt	
2	Mutual funds		Bills	
3	Stocks & bonds		Car loans	
4	RRSPs		Other loans	
5	Cash value ins.		Mortgages	
6	DC pension			
7	DB pension			
8	House			
9	Vehicles			
10	Toys			
	Total: A	$ xxx,xxx	Total: B	$ xx,xxx

Net Worth = Column (A) Total – Column (B) Total

Our key objective is to increase our net worth over time. This is our retirement pot or nest egg, and it represents our financial freedom. Calculate a Net Worth Statement at *least* once per year and at the *same time* each year.

Gather investment statements, property value assessments, and bank account balances, that is, all your financial data. A good time to complete or update a net worth statement is at each year-end. Setting financial goals for the next year at the same time as New Year's resolutions are made is a good idea.

We can grow our net worth in one of three ways:

1. Paying down our debts
2. Saving and adding funds into our investments
3. Market growth or appreciation of our assets

Those of us fortunate enough to own homes in Canada over the last decade saw an increase in our net worth strictly from an increase in the value of our real estate. We are all keenly aware that assets can depreciate or erode in value. The car purchased last year is not worth what it was a year ago and we are well aware from our property assessments and recent investment statements that real estate and stock values can erode.

We can't sit back and wait for appreciating assets to change our financial picture – that's out of our hands. We can *actively* create an increase in net worth by paying down our debts as well as by growing our savings. Better yet, especially as we approach our retirement objective, think long and hard before taking on any new debt!

Quality of Our Assets

Calculating our net worth statement is not all there is to the exercise although it is a good first step. We must analyze what the statement is telling us. To be most useful, this analysis needs to be done on a regular basis and we need to note the year-over-year changes. We need to view our own financial snapshot in the same way we would view a company we were considering investing in.

What assets does Heather Inc. hold? What is the calibre or quality of those assets? Are they long-life appreciating assets (good quality stocks, investment real estate), or are they depreciating assets (recreation vehicles, dirt bikes) that go down in value over time? Do the assets absorb income (recreation property, a gas-guzzling truck), or do these assets produce income (rental properties, dividend-paying stocks)?

There is nothing inherently wrong with an income-absorbing asset but we do have to look at how many income-absorbing assets we can afford to carry. When we retire, we want to reduce the assets that absorb income and those that don't appreciate in value. Go through your own assets and note by each of them whether they are income absorbing or generating, the approximate amount they generate or absorb, and whether they are appreciating or depreciating.

If you participate in a company pension plan, you will want to note these assets on the statement. For Defined Contribution plans, enter the present value of the account (assuming you are vested in the plan). For a Defined Benefit plan use the "termination" value or lump sum that you would be entitled to take with you if you left the company tomorrow. For details on these plans, see the chapter on company pension plans.

Net Worth Statement

Many life insurance policies do not build a cash value so there is no asset to record. Check your most recent annual policy statement from the insurance company. It will show the cash value, if any, of the policy.

Recreation Properties

For many, owning a second home in a sun belt or a recreation property is a retirement goal. I personally favour income-producing assets rather than a second home or recreation property. Many recreation properties are occupied less than 90 nights a year (less than 25% occupancy). If we look at the cost of operating a property such as utilities, property taxes, condo fees, roof replacement, carpet upgrades, painting, and so on, it likely runs better than $12,000 per year. That works out to more than $130 per night. In some parts of the globe, that amount can rent a very nice room with someone else doing the cleaning and maintenance!

Having said that, it ignores all the other important reasons one might choose to own a property, including possible appreciation, and providing a family gathering place. Part of this decision is an understanding of who you are.

I won't own a second residence until my husband Dennis has a lobotomy. When we are in one place, Dennis would be worried about the other property. Did he remember to turn down the heat on the hot water tank, was that furnace actually working? He would have a laundry list of things to fret about and that would interfere with our day-to-day relationship and ultimately our quality of life! On the other hand, I would face concerns over where to generate the additional month-to-month cash flow the property would require.

Our Home

There is an ongoing debate whether your own home should actually appear on the Net Worth statement if you are heading into retirement. We personally don't include our home because we choose to look only at the pot or nest egg that is available to feed and water us and send us travelling. Our house is our home and the roof over our head, which we don't intend to sell for the foreseeable future. Even if we were to sell, we would need to purchase something else with those funds.

Some of my clients did sell their big three or four bedroom family home in retirement, but very few actually took much money off the table to support their retirement lifestyle. When they purchased that new condo, they bought granite countertops, stainless steel appliances and a heated tile floor, and they couldn't take that ratty old couch from the family room in there. They had to have brand spanking new furniture and some new art for the walls. In the end, the amount they sold their house for ended up back in real estate and household possessions.

In the past, no one would retire while still carrying a mortgage. That's changing but in a perfect world, we won't carry *any* debts into retirement. Mortgage or debt payments of *any kind* require us to have greater retirement income in order to service the debt. If we are debt free, we get to retire earlier and/or to enjoy a higher cost retirement lifestyle.

I prefer to call our home "the last asset standing." If we own the roof over our head and we run out of retirement funds, we have an asset we can sell. The proceeds from the house can be used to keep us in an extended care facility or provide the comfort of knowing that there is a valuable asset to leave for the kids. Is it important to you to leave an estate? See more on that issue in the chapter on estate planning and insurance.

Many will protest that the house *should* be included on the Net Worth Statement. They'll assure me they *will* pull money off the table when they downsize or move to a less expensive community and they will take out a reverse mortgage to access the funds. Reverse mortgages are covered under personal savings and investments.

The Liability Picture

Looking at the debt or liability side of the Net Worth statement, we list our debts from the highest interest rate debt on down. For some, this will be the first time they've read the fine print to discover they are paying 24% on a department store credit card! Master Card and Visa are between 18% - 22% interest. Over time, we want to make sure we pay off the highest cost debts first and work our way down to the lower loan rate debts, including the mortgage.

There is actually no such thing as "good debt," but there is bad debt and better debt. Bad debt is debt where we cannot deduct the interest expense. In Canada, we can't deduct the interest expense of the mortgage against our income; it is an after tax item for us. In the United States, mortgage interest expense is deductible from income, which unfortunately creates a natural tendency to "over buy" or buy houses that are not really affordable.

In Canada, we can deduct interest expense if we borrow for investment purposes. If I borrow to buy a rental real estate property, the interest on the mortgage is deductible from my rental income and any excess is then deductible from my employment income.

If I borrow to purchase Royal Bank or any other stock, that also creates deductible-interest expense. Deductible-interest expense is certainly favoured over non-deductible interest expense, and our priority should be to pay off any non-deductible interest expense first.

From a tax standpoint, Canada Revenue Agency will allow us to rearrange our financial affairs in the most advantageous way possible. For example, if I own $60,000 in stocks (asset), and I have a $60,000 mortgage (liability), I can sell the stocks, pay off the mortgage, and later (at least 30 days forward) borrow $60,000 to re-buy the stock. By doing this, I have created deductible interest expense where previously I had non-deductible interest expense. I haven't changed my net worth statement at all but I am more tax efficient. Be sure to keep deductible and non-deductible loans *clearly* separate. Don't put both the kitchen renovation and the investment loan on the same line of credit or you risk CRA finding *all* of the interest expense non-deductible.

The "power pay" strategy is often used to help clients reduce their debt load more quickly. All debt except the highest rate debt is put on a minimum payment only and any extra funds are used to power pay as much as possible on the selected debt. When it is paid off, the same strategy is focused on the next debt.

Mortgage

If your mortgage is paid off, celebrate and skip this section. Give yourself a pat on the back while you're at it! Because mortgages are such an important issue, I want to deal with them just a little more.

None of these notions is rocket science. Pay your mortgage weekly as opposed to monthly. You can reduce the amortization period on the mortgage from 25 years down to less than 20 years just with that move. Increase your payment amount. Talk to your banker and discover the savings if you increased the payment from $975 to $1000. Double up a payment. Even if we doubled up only one payment a year, it would dramatically reduce the amount of time that it takes to clear the mortgage. Renew for a shorter amortization period.

Eliminating the mortgage prior to retirement leaves you with greater cash flow to spend on enjoyable activities. Little actions can accelerate the process. Based on a $200,000 five-year mortgage at 5.45% over 25 years, putting that $50 dinner or coffee and muffin equivalent on the mortgage each month will save $14,987 in interest costs and knock two years off the payments!

Drawing Down the Nest Egg

Our Net Worth Statement, our financial report card, represents a snapshot in time. How soon do we dip into our principle? The idea is to draw down the pot slowly. But how slowly? Most of us are *painfully* aware that even if we pick a conservative number like 5%, our retirement pot won't grow at a consistent 5% every year. Sometimes markets are up 11%, sometimes markets are down 30% percent (ouch), and sometimes they are flat. Stock market performance will cycle between good, bad, and ugly and our financial forecasts and drawdown rates have to take this into account.

Fidelity Investments did a study on a portfolio of 50% equities or stock, 35% bonds or fixed income, and 15% short-term instruments or cash. They assumed a constant rate of inflation of 2.25%. Their

Net Worth Statement

research shows you could withdraw 4% of the retirement pot in the first year and then increase withdrawals by the forecast 2.25% inflation rate each year and the money would last for your lifetime in 95% of the scenarios generated. There were 5% of scenarios where you would run out of money before you run out of life, but most of us would be pretty comfortable forecasting with a 95% probability.

Fidelity Investments are suggesting you can withdraw only $40,000 a year from a $1,000,000 pot to have a 95% percent certainty that the pot would last throughout your lifetime. If we need more than $40,000 a year, we can save a larger pot or we can take the risk and draw it down more aggressively. If we are paying close attention to the Net Worth Statement and recalculating it annually, we'll know if we are drawing the pot down too quickly and we can adjust the rate of drawdown.

Summary

In summary, we complete a Net Worth Statement each year leading up to our retirement, and each year *throughout* our retirement as well. If we experience a really poor year in the market and the value of our assets declines, we need to be aware of it and pull back on spending in the following year(s) or consider whether some part-time work or other alternative could help the situation. If we have been cautious in spending and assets have performed well, perhaps it's time to reward ourselves – with an eye to the future, of course!

A Net Worth worksheet and spreadsheet are available from our web site (www.retirementrocks.ca).

Net Worth Statement

To do: Life Design and Planning
            My Finances – Net Worth Statement

  * Evaluate appreciating / depreciating assets
  * Evaluate income absorbing / income generating assets
  * Identify deductible and non-deductible interest expense
  * Create a debt re-payment plan
  * Review retirement pot in each spouse's name

Finances

Cash Flow Statement

Happiness is a positive cash flow.

Fred Alder

Finances – Cash Flow Statement

In the last chapter, we looked at our nest egg. In this chapter, we look at another key part of the retirement equation – how much do you spend? An important part of any financial evaluation is to look at your personal cash flow statement. What cash comes in (your revenues) and what cash goes out (your expenses)? Getting a handle on cash flow is the *single largest factor within our control* regarding when retirement will be possible.

Sample Framework for Monthly Cash Flow Statement

	Income (cash in)	(A)	Spending (cash out)	(B)
	Revenues	$ amount	Expenses	$ amount
1	Employment income		Mortgage	
2	Bank interest		Personal loan	
3	Dividends		Utilities	

4	Rental property income		Property taxes	
5	Part-time work		Credit card payments	
6	Sale of assets		Food & drug costs	
7	Defined-benefit Pension		Insurance (home & car)	
8	CPP and/or OAS income		Entertainment	
9			Vehicle operating costs	
10				
11				
12				
	Total: A	$ xx,xxx	Total: B	$ xx,xxx

Net Free Cash Flow = Column (A) Total – Column (B) Total

Revenues

First look at revenues. For most of us that means our current employment income. In retirement, it would be great if we could create multiple sources of revenue. Even during our working life, it's a healthy option to have multiple sources of revenue. Consider employment income, interest income and dividend income from investments, rental income from investment properties, and income from part-time work. In retirement, income may be included from our company pension plan, government benefits and from self-employment earnings.

Cash Flow Statement

If we have multiple sources of revenue, then we have a little more insulation against negative events affecting the value of our investment portfolio. It's important to look at the revenues or incomes that will come into each partner's name (more on that under income splitting). We also consider the timeline for revenues for each of us. The retirement age in the example below is 58 years.

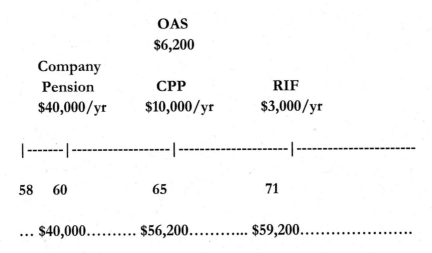

When am I going to retire? When is my spouse going to retire? Will I/we retire fully or continue to work part-time? Have we both contributed to CPP? When will I/we take CPP (early at age 60 or age 65 or 70)? Do I/we qualify for OAS (age 65)? When can I/we begin to take pension income (if any)?

Are there other sources of retirement income available such as rent from investment properties or pensions from other countries? When will conversion of LIRAs to LIFs or RSPs to RIFs be done (mandatory by age 71)?

The retirement "alphabet soup" is covered in further chapters. Is there an inheritance expected? How much is it and when might it happen? What do I anticipate my life expectancy to be?

If you retire at 55, what are you going to do between 55 and 60 for income or between age 60 and 65? What new sources of income will be added at each point along the way?

Expenses

Next is a long, hard look at our expenses. What are we currently spending our money on? Financial freedom is created *not through what we earn* but by *what we keep*. We can't grow net worth unless we have net free cash flow to direct towards investments. If we ask a group of people approaching retirement "How many of you have $10,000 left over at the end of the year?" the answer is probably no one.

Many are financially past the days when we had to count the nickels and dimes to make it to month-end, but now we don't count the dollars either. Most of us simply allow our spending to expand to use *all* the available funds. A study that was released by Mackenzie Investments in January 2006 showed spend-happy Canadians have a tough time making $100 cash last the workweek. Most Canadians frittered away the funds in four days and others burned through it in 48 hours. Burning through $100 every four days works out to $760 per month. This cash could be invested, saved or used to pay down debt or go toward experiences you really value. Frittering is no fun! It's certainly not my place to "should" on anyone and to tell you what it's OK or not OK to spend your money on. Spend money on the things that bring you pleasure and add joy or beauty and juice to your life, but be mindful and exercise choice in your spending.

Cash Flow Statement

Whoever told you *"You can have it all"* obviously had no plans for retirement!

An awareness of daily spending is the greatest gift my Depression-era mother gave her children. She believed that if you looked after the pennies, the dollars would look after themselves. When my father retired, he loved to scan the grocery flyers and let my mother know where the best weekly buys were so eventually she put him in charge of grocery shopping. That was a careful, coupon-clipping generation. Perhaps we will all learn a more frugal outlook too. One of my girlfriends takes great delight in her Value Village wardrobe finds.

Those pennies add up! Paying $1 per bottle of water twice a day for a family of four adds up to $2,920 a year. Invest that in a tax-deferred account instead and earn 7%, and 25 years later that's $175,401.38! Tap water is free and environmentally friendlier. If each of you purchases a paperback a month for $11.99, you've spent $287.76 a year. Invested as above that's $18,777.34.[1] A library card in most major centers is less than $20 annually and gives you access to DVDs, CDs, books on tape for that next car trip and all the latest bestsellers.

When was the last time you actually tracked your daily spending? Was it years ago, or perhaps never? Track *every* expense for one month, or better yet a full calendar quarter. "How much do you spend?" will be among the first questions any financial advisor asks. Without knowing your personal *"burn rate,"* any forecasting you do on retirement needs will be garbage in and garbage out. In Life Design and Planning you'll find a cash flow statement that can be used to begin tracking spending now!

1. Fidelity Investments "Getting You There" Newsletter, Winter 2007-08

Cash Flow Statement

I asked clients who were anticipating retirement to create three separate scenarios for me. Look first at what it costs to feed, water, and house you with *none* of life's extras. This is Chicken Little's "the sky is falling" spending level. Then I asked them to give me their full and complete "enough" picture. I wanted their personal, *believable* version of the "lifestyles of the rich and famous." If their normal life ambitions didn't include a villa in France, I didn't want them adding it in now. My "lifestyles" picture includes entertaining at home, travel, funds to try new hobbies, and maintaining my cleaning person and personal trainer. I have no desire for yachts or for new cars every three years.

Finally, I wanted clients to tell me what they would be prepared to discard if they had to. I asked them to show me a life more than the minimalist picture but less than the full-meal deal. I would still entertain for special holidays but perhaps less frequently than I do now or perhaps pasta would make a more frequent menu appearance. I could take my big trip every second year or third year or regretfully forgo it altogether. Just don't ask me to lose the cleaning person!

These numbers represent your "burn rate." The next part of the exercise is to calculate how large a retirement pot each of these burn rates would require using the 20 times or 25 times spending estimate.

We don't directly control the market value of our portfolios or the property taxes on our present home or the current cost of a loaf of bread. *We do have control* over what we choose to spend money on. As an "acid test," I asked my clients to practise living on what they told me they could live on for at least six months leading up to their retirement!

Cash Flow Statement

Many financial planners will assume that provided you have no debts, your home is fully paid for and your children are self-sufficient, you could retire on two-thirds to three-quarters of your working income. That is just an estimate. The most accurate number comes from your own tracking. Each of us is different and so our vision of retirement and the way we spend our time differs. This is why the visioning exercise is so important and it needs to come first!

My clients tended to spend *more* in their first two years of retirement than previously, but reduced spending once they had settled into their chosen retirement lifestyle. Early years typically involved greater travel and sprucing up the homestead. As clients aged, they had fewer material wants and travel and recreation expenses dropped. Our generation is likely to be responsible for a greater share of our own healthcare expenses.

Which of our expenses will decrease in retirement? If the mortgage and consumer debts are paid off, we don't need extra cash flow to cover them. We can reduce expenses if the kids are off the payroll. Dennis and I tease, *with love*, that it's time we entered the parents' protection program and moved away with no forwarding address. Perhaps it's time, as a recent television commercial promotes, to stop cooking with cheese!

Car expenses may be reduced because we no longer drive to work. Consider becoming a one-car household in retirement. Walking more would serve some health objectives too!

Our "home" wardrobe may not require dry cleaning like a work wardrobe. I refuse to own garments that can't survive my laundry regime. We no longer have deductions for Canada Pension Plan, Employment Insurance, or Company Pension Plans. There are no group insurance premiums, and we are no longer setting aside funds for retirement.

That's one of the greatest psychological adjustments Dennis and I had to make. Rather than adding funds into the retirement pot, we were supposed to take it out! When you've had 40 or more years of earning money and increasing savings, it's hard to feel good about taking it out. I'm pleased to report we are getting better at it!

Which of our expenses do we foresee increasing? Leisure activities will be more expensive and so will travel and possibly healthcare. We may need to pay more for medical insurance or personal care, and we may want to help the children or grandchildren or even our aging parents.

Get a handle on the spending area of your financial life and you will write the script for your financial freedom.

Managing Finances

My father was an electrician. He worked at his trade for more than 40 years. For the most part, I believe that he was happy with his work and gained a reasonable amount of satisfaction from it day-to-day. The first 25 years of his working life phase was with a coal mining company that went bankrupt in the 1950s. At that point, his accumulated pension earnings disappeared. In those days, pension plans were generally not fully funded or protected by any kind of legislation. For the next 20 years, he was employed by a small neon sign company that had no pension plan. He and my mother arrived at retirement age having raised four children on a meagre tradesman's salary with few savings and income from OAS and CPP. He was debt free and the mortgage was paid off. He chose a

Cash Flow Statement

modest lifestyle within his means that enabled him to be happy and to do just fine financially during his retirement.

Wisdom From the Trenches

Leading up to retirement, most of us concentrate on finances. We have a goal to work toward. Here's some wisdom from the trenches.

Dennis and I operate under the "windfall rule." Any time money comes into our hands that was not anticipated (NO, income tax refunds aren't a windfall), one third went to the past for debt repayment, one third went to the future for savings, and one third went to the present for special indulgences. The income tax refund went to savings or the mortgage!

Hand in hand with that was another principle we operated by. We had a firm agreement that *neither* of us would spend more than $500 without consulting the other and gaining his or her agreement, even if we viewed the funds as coming from our "own" money. The amount may vary with household incomes but the principle shouldn't be ignored. Perhaps those with deeper pockets would agree on a few thousand dollars, those with more limited circumstances perhaps less than $100. The agreement acknowledged that we *both* had a stake and a contribution to make to our financial future and that we are "partners" in the broadest definition of that term. Too many people blame their partner's spending as the reason they can't make financial headway! Perhaps it's time to put some financial *partnership principles* in place!

Cleaning out a lifetime of accumulation for my in-laws when they moved into an extended-care facility led to another promise; actually that *and* our Costco membership! If something new comes into our house, something like it has to leave. Go ahead and buy a new pair of shoes or that hard-to-resist deal on Costco T-shirts but which pair of shoes or which T-shirt are you committing to send to Goodwill? At 50+ years of age just how much more "stuff" does it take to make us happy? Travelling to third-world countries is a great eye-opener. North Americans lead more than lives of abundance. In many instances, we lead lives of excess. More *stuff* will not make you happy. The simpler we make our lives, the more abundant they become.

A study conducted by Professor Ryan Howell, a psychologist at San Francisco State University, concluded that people who spend money on simple experiences such as the theatre, dining out or taking adventure holidays tend to be happier than those who buy material possessions, regardless of how much they spend. "Memories of life experiences gave people a greater sense of vitality and being alive than material items."

If you have things to give away or items you are looking for, check out Freecycle (freecycle.org). Members give away unwanted items in order to keep useful items out of landfills. You can also contact charitable organizations in your area and donate gently used clothing or household items to help others. Your business clothes can help others get a professional start.

While I am concerned about the global financial situation, I can't help but feel these events are likely to bring a welcome and needed re-evaluation of our values and our lifestyle. That's not a bad thing. Lunch out is a nice "date" and cost less than dinner out. Growing a vegetable garden is a meaningful pursuit for many. Family game or movie night with the grandchildren at home builds connection.

Cash Flow Statement

Financial freedom lies in managing your resources well. We are enjoying that freedom and wouldn't choose to return to full-time work even for the promise of more to spend. We have *"enough."*

A Cash Flow worksheet and spreadsheet are available from our web site (www.retirementrocks.ca).

To do: Life Design and Planning
            My Finances - Cash Flow Statement

   * Estimate retirement living expenses
   * Create a purchasing plan of big-ticket items pre-retirement
   * Draft income timeline and review income splitting

Finances

Company Pensions

*Chase your passion
not your pension.*

Denis Waitley

Company Pensions

Registered Pension Plans

The Office of the Superintendent of Financial Institutions reported in 2007 that less than 25 percent of Canadian workers are covered by a company pension plan. There are two basic types of Registered Pension Plans, *Defined Benefit* and *Defined Contribution*. In both plans, the intent is to provide income during retirement, income for our survivors should we predecease them, and a termination value if we should "love and leave" the company before retirement.

Defined Benefit or DB Plan

Defined Benefit Pension plans are most often found with federal, provincial or municipal government employers and much less frequently in private industry. These plans are less and less common in Canada because they are complicated and costly to administer, and companies can't control their cost to provide the benefit.

With a DB plan, the end-game benefit can be known because it's based on a formula that includes years of service and level of earnings. With a Defined Benefit Pension, we know exactly how much retirement income we have to work with and the comfort of knowing that this is payable for our lifetime.

If we are married or in a common-law relationship, our partner will be entitled to a reduced pension on our passing, typically 60% (slightly higher in Manitoba) of our benefit. The assumption is that if there is just one of us turning on the lights and eating groceries, the household cost of living would fall. If we are both hit by a truck and pass away, there may be no estate or residual value unless the plan has a guaranteed payment period (commonly 10 years for a single person, with no guarantee, unless purchased, for a couple).

The Termination Value shown on a Pension Statement is the amount to be included when calculating your Net Worth. Your company will have resources you can use or in-house projection programs where you can calculate your anticipated retirement income.

On Retirement (DB Plan)

Most Defined Benefit plan members will elect to take a monthly income under the pension plan and the cheque will arrive in their bank account each month after retirement. If you retire before your normal retirement date, as defined by your plan, you may have the option of taking a reduced, immediate benefit or deferring the payments and taking an unreduced payment at a later date.

Another option that is often presented is to take the commuted value of the plan and transfer it to a Locked-In Retirement Account in your name (LIRA). The Income Tax Act puts a limit on the amount that can be transferred to a LIRA and any amounts over the cap are received as taxable income unless you have RRSP contribution room available. Carefully consider your willingness to take on the investment management and any additional Defined Benefit Plan features you may forgo with this option.

Defined Contribution or DC Plan

A Defined Contribution Pension, sometimes called a Money Purchase plan, defines the contributions that are going into the plan. Contributions are usually based on a percentage of salary and the percentage contribution may increase with greater years of service with the company. The company is the contributor and may allow for optional voluntary contributions by the employee and/or they may offer a contribution-matching program. Companies prefer DC plans because their cost is fixed and known. A DC plan is also easier to set up and less costly and complicated to administer.

What is not known is how much retirement income the plan will generate when we retire. The income question is based on the contributions to the plan and the investment return that will be achieved through our investment decisions over the life of the plan.

One of the biggest advantages of a Defined Contribution plan is that it has estate or residual value. Touch wood, if we were to get hit by a Mac truck, the funds under our DC umbrella pass to our named beneficiaries (tax free to a spouse or dependant child).

DC plans often allow for greater personal RRSP contribution room. The present value of the DC plan, as shown on a company-issued Pension Statement, is the amount to be included in your Net Worth calculations.

The company or a service provider may have projection programs that allow you to calculate the likely growth on Defined Contribution pension assets, given an expected rate of return and continuing contributions. Some future value tables are included in Life Design and Planning for you to estimate values yourself.

At the end of the day, either by leaving the company to work elsewhere or through retiring, we will walk away with an umbrella of money, provided we are vested (usually two years or less).

There are administrative processes and a time lag between leaving the company and getting the first withdrawal from a LIF. It could be as long as three months. We need to be sure to plan for another source of funds to live on before expecting to get at that LIF money.

Send Me Money Honey

Defined Contribution plan members and those Defined Benefit members who choose to take the Commuted Value of their plans will arrange for a transfer of their funds away from their employer to their choice of financial services company, where they will hold the funds in an umbrella called a LIRA (Locked-In Retirement Account) or Locked-In RRSP (the terms are virtually synonymous). We need to pay attention to the *locked* designation because this indicates there are rules involved in getting your hands on the money.

If we have gone on to work for a new employer and don't need income from these funds, we'll just let that umbrella continue to grow, tax sheltered.

When we are ready to generate retirement income, we can choose to use the proceeds under the LIRA umbrella to purchase a life annuity (covered below) or we can continue to manage our investments and transfer the funds to a Life Income Fund (LIF), Locked-In Retirement Income Fund (LRIF – Manitoba, Newfoundland) or Prescribed RRIF (PRIF – Saskatchewan, Manitoba).

The "F" in these account names indicates we have elected income and turned on the income *faucet*. The faucet can be turned on generally at minimum age 55 (50 Alberta) and *must* be turned on before we reach age 71. This is a restricted flow faucet because these plans have minimum withdrawals like RRIFs but are also covered by *maximum* allowable withdrawal rules.

A maximum withdrawal chart is shown in Life Design and Planning. LIFs and related options do not provide for any automatic cost-of-living adjustments. We protect ourselves against inflation through the investments we choose.

Once we've turned the faucet on in an LIF, we must take money out at least annually but can choose monthly, quarterly or semi-annually. Our desired payment frequency may influence the type of investments we hold. If we want monthly payments, we can't hold Guaranteed Investment Certificates that mature in one year or longer, and it becomes more challenging to hold individual equities.

Early Access to Funds

In most provinces across Canada, when we transfer the money from a LIRA to a life annuity or LIF, we can unlock from 25% to 50% of the value of the account on a one-time basis and shift this money over to our regular RRSP or take it into our hands as taxable income.

I will unlock funds when the time comes because I don't like rules and I like to stay flexible. I don't want to be limited by government regulations on minimum/maximum withdrawal. An important factor is that permission is needed from our "pension partner" or spouse to do this unlocking.

There are other ways to get at the funds in the locked-in umbrella. These are shortened life expectancy, severe financial hardship, or in some jurisdictions, we can be forced to unlock the plan for awards for maintenance enforcement, either spousal or child support.

If we leave the country and become a non-resident, we may also be able to unlock the plan. Any time funds are taken from under the tax-sheltered umbrella, they are subject to income tax.

We own the funds under the LIRA or LIF umbrellas and at the time of our death, the whole umbrella will be transferred to our named beneficiary. Funds continue tax-sheltered if left to a spouse (dependant child or grandchild), but will be taxed if left to adult children or another beneficiary.

Annuities

Rather than choosing a LIRA and then an LIF, we may choose to purchase a life annuity with the funds from our DC Pension. In essence, our umbrella of funds is "sold" to a life insurance company in exchange for a monthly income that will last for our lifetime. It is possible to transfer a portion of the funds to an LIF and use the balance for an annuity. We can move funds from an LIF to an annuity but an annuity decision is final.

If married or in a common-law relationship, a joint life annuity must be chosen so that 60 % or more of our monthly income will be paid to the spouse for his or her lifetime upon our death. In the absence of a purchased guarantee, if both get hit by a truck, the income will end with no estate value.

Payments will be based on life expectancy and current interest rates. Because of differences in life expectancy, a woman will receive a smaller monthly payment, assuming the same-sized pot, than a man of the same age. A sample payout schedule is shown in Life Design and Planning.

Some annuities may allow for the purchase of a cost-of-living adjustment but it will be costly.

Health, Dental and Life Insurance

At retirement, we will no longer participate in company savings plans nor will we have the short-term or long-term disability coverage that we may have had with the company. We may also lose any extended medical and dental coverage, and life and accident insurance.

We are often allowed to convert company life insurance coverage into personal coverage within 31 days of leaving the company. We first need to consider whether we need the insurance, and, second, whether we can purchase it for less cost elsewhere. The advantage of converting company insurance is that often no medical evidence of insurability is required.

Be sure to review available retiree benefits with human resource personnel.

Company Savings Plans, Group RRSPs

Many companies do not provide a pension program. Some do not offer any programs for encouraging retirement savings; some may offer group RRSPs or other similar plans.

This book deals with these other savings in the Personal Savings chapter. We need not let the absence of a company program deter us from creating our own financial plan for our retirement!

To do: Review Company Plans and Retirement Benefits

Finances

Government Benefits

The desire of gold is not for gold,
it is for the means of freedom and benefit.

Ralph Waldo Emerson

Government Benefits

Canada Pension Plan/Quebec Pension Plan (CPP/QPP)

Let's look at other sources of income over and above the company pension plan, starting with the Canada Pension Plan/Quebec Pension Plan or CPP/QPP. Employers and individuals each pay into this program throughout their working lives to a set amount of maximum pensionable earnings each year. Self-employed individuals contribute double in order to cover both employee and employer portions.

Some clients worry that these funds would not be there for them when they retired. I have no idea how the program may change for future generations but changes made in 1998 to increase contribution rates and change the investment strategy have put the program back on track.

The Canada Pension Plan is intended primarily as a retirement pension, but it can provide us with a disability pension if we are disabled during our working years or survivors' benefits to our spouse and/or dependant children if we die. There is also a lump-sum death benefit but before your survivors go planning a splashy funeral, you should know it's been frozen at just $2,500. One of my clients said, "That's not enough to get me planted!"

Details on these benefits can be found at servicecanada.gc.ca (look under Seniors). You must file an application in order to receive benefits.

Maximum Benefits

For 2009, the maximum retirement benefit payable at age 65 is $10,905 a year or $909 per month. It is indexed annually for inflation and is received as a taxable benefit. If you were a homemaker and did not work outside the home then you will not be entitled to a CPP/QPP benefit.

CPP/QPP can be taken as early as age 60 provided you have "substantially ceased working." The website provides an explanation. Early pension will be discounted by 0.5% per month or 6% per year. This equates to 30% less income, $7,634 in 2009 at age 60. If you choose to delay retirement, you can increase it by 6% per year for up to 30% more at age 70. I have to confess that of the hundreds of clients I dealt with over the years, not one chose to take it later. They couldn't wait to get their hands on that government benefits cheque!

Drop Out Years

The CPP retirement benefit is calculated on the number of years you contributed as well as the level of contributions. In calculating an eligible individual's benefit amount, Canada Pension Plan/QPP will automatically "drop out" or eliminate 15% of their lowest-income years and will also drop out any years that individual may have been on CPP disability.

If you were the primary caregiver, you can apply to drop the years where you had low or no income and were caring for children under the age of seven under the Child Rearing Provision. You must apply and provide birth certificates – this is one area frequently missed.

Where income splitting for tax purposes is advantageous, you can assign your spouse part of your benefit calculated *during the years you were together* provided you have both reached age 60. An ex-spouse can apply to share the CPP/QPP earned during the years you were married.

It is a good idea to request a Canada Pension Plan/QPP estimate prior to retiring so you'll have an idea of the income from this source. You can phone 1-800-277-9914 or apply for an estimate on the website (servicecanada.gc.ca) under Seniors. You will need your Social Insurance Number (SIN).

Note: May 25, 2009, the Minister of Finance proposed changes to the CPP Program that, if passed by Parliament, will come into force in 2011. Proposals will remove the Work Cessation test for those taking benefits at age 60, marginally improve the percent of "drop-out" years, and will increase the penalty to 6% per month for those taking early benefits (36% at age 60).

Government Benefits - Old Age Security

Old Age Security or OAS is available to Canadian citizens or landed immigrants; there is no requirement to have worked in Canada to qualify. There are, however, specific residence requirements. OAS will not begin until age 65 with no option to take it earlier. Maximum OAS income is $6,204 a year (Jan 2009) or $517 a month. It is taxable income and is adjusted to inflation each calendar quarter.

One of my well-heeled clients said, "Oh who cares? It's barely enough to pay for my wine." I knew then he was drinking better wine than I do!

Seniors Claw Back

OAS is a *means*-tested program subject to the "seniors claw-back." The government begins to take back the funds when your net income from all sources exceeds a base amount of $66,335 and they take it all back if net income exceeds approximately $107,000 (2009 numbers). Payments will be reduced at source, based on your previous year's income tax return. Only about 5% of OAS recipients are affected by claw-backs with just 2% losing the entire benefit.

The claw-back may have us learning more about income splitting options, planning RRSP withdrawals more carefully, taking CPP/QPP earlier, and planning how to divest ourselves of assets in retirement.

I had clients who owned five rental properties. If they chose to sell one property a year for five years, chances are they would experience full OAS claw-back for each year. If they sold all properties at once, they'd certainly experience claw-back for that year, but they would continue to receive OAS for the other years. They also had an option to sell the properties before age 65. Clearly, the sale of any asset has more considerations than OAS claw-back but it warrants consideration.

OAS is paid from general government revenues and is one of the most expensive federal programs to run. In the future, I think it is likely we will see changes to this program. OAS payments will not start arriving in your mailbox automatically; initiate your applications for both CPP and OAS four to six months ahead of time.

Further details can be found at (servicecanada.gc.ca).

Government Benefits – Other Programs

Other government assistance may be available under the umbrella of the OAS program for eligible low-income Canadians such as Guaranteed Income Supplement (GIS), and Spousal Allowance (SA). These programs are generally non-taxable and means-tested annually.

If a couple each receives maximum OAS and CPP, they could have income of approximately $34,000 per year at age 65. That may be sufficient to replace a family income of approximately $50,000 a year pre-tax with no further savings. Many of us choose to retire sooner and may have plans for a costlier lifestyle. In the absence of a company pension plan, greater personal savings will be required.

To do: Order a CPP Statement of Contributions

Finances

Personal Savings and Investments

*An investment in knowledge
always pays the best interest.*

Benjamin Franklin

Personal Savings and Investments

Most of us know that at this point, the buck stops here. Even if we are fortunate enough to have a company pension, we've got to do some aggressive savings of our own. We start with tax-sheltered vehicles such as RRSPs, spousal RRSPs and the newly introduced Tax Free Savings Accounts (TFSA).

If we can shelter our investments from tax, the investment pool can grow faster. We then invest in non-sheltered savings and investment accounts that invest in the most tax-efficient way possible.

For those with higher incomes and no company pension plans, the reality is that we can't save enough to support our preferred retirement lifestyles exclusively with RRSP accounts that we waited until we were 30+ years of age to get serious about. In David Chilton's popular book, "The Wealthy Barber," he calls for savings of 10% per year. Provided you started that discipline in your younger years, giving plenty of time for compounding returns on the investment, a 10% savings rate may have been sufficient.

During my years as an advisor, I met numerous individuals very good at spending money, but fewer that were really good savers. Many sacrificed *future* choices to big houses, nice wardrobes, dinners out and great holidays *today*. They arrived at 50+ years of age wanting to know how *I* could get them retired in the next few years because they wanted that *too*! I couldn't, and they were in need of a reality check and an abrupt change in behaviour.

We discussed in the "How Much is Enough" chapter how important it is to sit down regularly with an advisor to do financial forecasting, and/or regularly completing one for yourself using the resources I recommended. Even if the news isn't what you hoped for, playing ostrich won't change the outcome. The "best" time to begin your savings program was when you were 20; the next best time is NOW. If the outcome of your forecasts is encouraging, give yourself an "atta boy or atta girl"! If the outcome is not what you hoped for, then the rubber needs to hit the road *now*.

Tax Free Savings Accounts (TFSA)

The federal budget in 2008 gave *all* Canadians a terrific gift that made savings and income splitting easier. Beginning January 2009, investors 18 or older are eligible to open a tax-free savings account and will be allowed to contribute up to $5,000 per year. Contributions are NOT tax deductible, unlike RRSP contributions. If you are still working and in a higher tax bracket, it is more advantageous to make maximum RRSP contributions before you start a TFSA. In a perfect world you will do both.

Like your RRSP, you can invest your funds in a savings account, GIC, stocks, bonds or mutual funds. We get tax incentives to hold equities and dividend-paying stocks in taxable accounts via capital gains tax treatment and dividend tax credits. These new accounts are a good place to hold bonds and GICs because interest income is ordinarily heavily taxed.

Beware of fees. Some firms are charging administration fees as well as withdrawal fees. Look for no-fee deals in the account's early days. These account fees (as well as any interest expenses for borrowing funds to invest) are NOT tax deductible for a TFSA (also true for RRSPs).

The big payoff for these accounts comes over the long haul. Don't use them as short-term piggy banks. If you contribute $200 a month for 20 years at an average annual return of 5.5% you will accumulate $11,045 *more* than you would in a taxable account. The investment growth or returns earned under the umbrella grow and compound free of tax and there is no taxation on withdrawal of the growth or of the initial contribution. You are able to re-contribute withdrawals and access funds without affecting eligibility for federally sponsored benefits such as OAS. Contribution room can be carried forward for future years (like the RRSP). While $5,000 isn't a large sum, ten years from now, you will be able to shelter earnings on $50,000. Now that's very useful!

Those of us already retired or shortly headed into retirement should be using these accounts to shift assets held in non-sheltered taxable investments into TFSAs as our contribution room permits. If we make "in kind" contributions of shares or other investments we already own, we will have to claim taxable capital gains on the contribution and will lose the ability to deduct the capital losses – just as with "in kind" RRSP contributions. Like an RRSP, when a capital loss is realized in a TSFA, it cannot be used to offset taxable capital gains.

These accounts really shine as a solid income-splitting opportunity. See additional comments in the chapter titled Income Splitting.

From an estate perspective, there is a deemed disposition on the death of the TFSA holder but it is tax-free, making the estate larger than if these funds were held in a taxable account. TFSA clients can generally name a "successor holder" (only a spouse or common-law partner) or "beneficiary" on the account but check that the appropriate legislation to do so has been passed in your province *or* be sure your intentions are indicated in your will.

RRSPs and RRIFs

Registered Retirement Savings Plans are another tax-sheltered umbrella most Canadians are familiar with. Over our working life, we are permitted to contribute each year up to 18% of our previous year's earned income minus our Pension Adjustment (for those who are part of company plans) to a maximum of $21,000 (for 2009).

We are able to deduct the RRSP contribution from taxable income. The money under the RRSP umbrella compounds tax-sheltered for many years, ideally until we make withdrawals to fund retirement. You can reach under that umbrella at any time and withdraw funds but if you do so, that cash is added to your taxable income in the year of withdrawal. You don't need to convert your RRSP to a RRIF (Registered Retirement Income Fund) account in order to get access to this money. That's where the RRSP is unlike LIRAs or Locked-In accounts where you *must* convert to a LIF in order to access funds.

You may convert your RRSP to a RRIF at any time but cannot delay that conversion past age 71. Once converted, you must take a minimum withdrawal each year but there is no maximum withdrawal. You'll remember the RRIF is the income option because of the *F* in the name. You've turned on the income *faucet*.

The 2008 federal budget introduced new rules for income splitting with your spouse. That budget change may make it advantageous for couples to RRIF at age 64 (rather than wait until 71) in order to make your first withdrawal at 65. You can income split RRIF withdrawals starting at age 65. You will find more on this topic in the chapter on income splitting. You may also use this income to take advantage of the $2,000 Pension Income Tax Credit (assuming you have no company plan).

RRIFs are offered by all financial institutions. They are really just your RRSP account with a new label. You can hold exactly the same investments in your RRIF that you held in the RRSP. See the table in Life Design and Planning showing minimum withdrawals.

If there is an advantage to making smaller withdrawals (you don't need the income) you can do so by basing your withdrawals on your younger spouse's age. The withdrawal is added to your taxable income for the year but only on withdrawals over the minimum will the financial institution withhold tax before sending your payment.

When opening an RRIF, be sure to fill in the beneficiary designation because this doesn't automatically transfer over from the RRSP account. If you die having named your spouse as the beneficiary of your RRIF, your spouse can continue exactly the same payment schedule from your plan or s/he can move the funds to his or her own RRSP or RRIF or to an annuity. These will be tax-free rollovers. The spouse could also cash it all in, pay tax on the income and take a trip.

If you've named an adult child as the beneficiary, the remainder of the account is cashed out and your estate must pay the tax just as if you had withdrawn it all prior to your death. Special treatment will apply when naming dependant children or grandchildren as beneficiaries

Spousal RRSPs and RRIFs

My RRSP contribution room is based on *my* earned income and I may choose to invest all the funds in my own RRSP *or* some in mine and some in an RRSP account in Dennis' name, called a spousal RRSP. Opening a spousal RRSP does not interfere with Dennis' own contribution room (provided he has earned income). The advantage of directing contributions to Dennis' name is that this income will be taxed in his hands in retirement. There is more on these accounts under Income Splitting.

Annuities

Rather than, or in addition to opening a RRIF to provide for retirement income, you can use some or all of the funds accumulated in your RRSP to purchase an annuity. As we learned in the chapter on company pensions, an annuity is a contract with an insurance company (plus banks or credit unions in the case of a fixed term) whereby I exchange my investment funds for a monthly income. This means I don't have the pool of investments any more so I can't dip into it for extraordinary expenses.

With RRSP funds you may purchase an annuity payable for your lifetime (and that of your spouse) or a fixed-term annuity to age 90.

Caution – many of us will live beyond 90! Any time we add a bell or a whistle to the contract, we will receive a lower monthly payment from the outset; for example, a guarantee it will pay me or my estate for 10 years, or give my spouse 75% or 100% instead of 60% of my benefit should I die, or provide inflation adjustments to the payment.

A life annuity guarantees an income for your lifetime (and that of your spouse) but the benefit "dies" with you, leaving no estate value in the absence of a purchased guarantee. These are interest-rate sensitive investments. If we lock in at a low rate, it stays that way for the life of the contract. The payments out of the plan are all taxed as income.

We have covered the tax-sheltering opportunities available through company Pension Plans, Registered Retirement Savings Plans (RRSP) and Tax Free Savings Accounts (TFSA). Once we have used the full advantages these accounts offer, our only other recourse is to save and invest as tax-efficiently as possible.

Tax Efficient Investing

Take a look at the Taxation chart in the appendix. This chart shows the *marginal* tax rates by province of the tax we pay on the last or highest dollar of income we earn.

The Federal Budget announcement of January, 2009 included an increase of 7.5% in the lowest income tax brackets. This is good news because it will lower the marginal tax rate for a good number of Canadians. If you are contemplating a move to another province in retirement, differing taxation levels are simply more data to consider.

Tax-bracket management through income splitting and/or making RRSP contributions is a big part of tax planning. So too are the principles of tax-efficient investing. What the charts tell you is that the higher the income in your name, the greater the tax you will pay. They also show that less tax is paid on capital gains and dividends than on interest income.

Interest income is earned from cash and fixed-income investing in vehicles such as treasury bills, bonds, bond mutual funds, GICs and interest-bearing savings accounts. We pay the same rate of tax on this source of investment income as we do on our paycheques – lots! It adds insult to injury that these investments are paying historically low rates *and* we pay the highest rate of tax on this income.

Capital gains occur when we sell any capital investment for a price greater than we paid for it. This can be real estate investments, stocks (equities), or bonds. If I paid $10 for something that I sell for $20, I have earned a $10 capital gain.

Capital losses are the reverse situation (I sell something for less than I paid for it). We may use our capital losses to offset our capital gains and we can carry capital losses back up to three years on our income tax returns to offset past gains. We can also carry losses forward indefinitely to offset future gains.

When claiming a capital gain we pay tax on only 50% of the gain, at our tax rate. We are taxed on just $5 of a $10 gain. That is an attractive incentive to own equities over fixed-income investments in taxable accounts! The sale of our *own* principal residence is the only tax-free capital gain most of us are allowed (the sale of a small Canadian business or farm property has special rules).

When we invest in shares of *Canadian* corporations that pay dividends, we receive special tax treatment on these dividends. Corporations pay tax on their income before paying out those dividends, so in order not to tax this income twice, the government initiated the Canadian Dividend Tax Credit. The result is less tax paid on dividends.

Generally speaking, when we invest in non-sheltered investment accounts, we want to favour investments that pay dividends and capital gains over interest-producing investments, especially if we are a higher-income earner. We may choose to hold those interest earning investments under the shelter of an RRSP or TFSA or in the hands of the lower-income earner.

If you hold a sizeable non-sheltered portfolio, it would benefit you to get specialized advice about these issues. Further useful information is available at www.taxtips.ca.

Reverse Mortgages

In previous generations, there was no darn way *anyone* was going to take out a reverse mortgage after spending a lifetime getting the dang house paid for! The fact is that our home does represent an asset that some may be required to draw on to fund retirement.

If I am mortgage-free and over 60 (65 for some lenders) I can go to a mortgage lending agency or reverse mortgage agency and they will give me a lump sum, or a monthly income (or a combination) based on the value of my home. If I live in a $500,000 house, most of the programs out there will give me 50% percent of the value, or $250,000. The interest clock starts as soon as I get the money. I'm not required to make payments, but the interest, of course, is compounding and accruing until either I pass away or I sell the house. Then I (or my estate) must pay the piper.

On a regular mortgage over the course of a 25-year amortization period, and ignoring appreciation, the house has been paid for two or three times simply through the interest costs alone. Of course a piece of the principal is also being paid down with each payment. You can imagine the amount owing on a higher-rate reverse mortgage where no principal repayments are being made! The financial disadvantages are clear but it allows you to stay in your own home and use that asset to fund retirement.

Summary

We have reviewed a number of sources of income you may have in retirement. You may have company pension plans, CPP and OAS from the federal government, your RRSP, TFSAs, Annuities, Reverse Mortgages, and other personal savings. Perhaps you have rental income from investment properties, or even farm income. If you have worked in another country, it's possible you may qualify for a foreign pension and should certainly look into that. You may have part-time or full-time employment income or you may start a business from home. We cover self-employment, contract and consulting work, and part-time employment in the chapter titled More Work or Volunteering.

Don't forget seniors' rates when shopping! My Scottish heritage obviously hasn't influenced Dennis much because I can't convince him to ask for the seniors' discount that is offered at age 55 in some stores. Perhaps when he is 60!

Finances

Tax Strategies in Retirement

*The hardest thing in the world to
understand is the income tax.*

Albert Einstein

Tax Strategies in Retirement

The Taxman Doesn't Retire!

Our tax world changes when we retire. Chances are you have had
tax and other deductions handled by your employer during your
working years. If you filed your own tax returns, you were perhaps
aware of issues like your personal and spousal exemptions and
deductions for RRSP contributions but had no need to keep an eye
on other tax issues such as age and pension income credits.

If you are receiving a Defined Benefit Pension your employer will
continue to remit income taxes based on that source of income but
chances are when we add all other sources of retirement income,
you may still owe additional tax. You can choose to have taxes
withheld at source from your CPP and OAS payments and from
RRIF withdrawals. There is no mechanism to have taxes withheld
from the interest and dividend income earned in non-sheltered
investment accounts or from rental income and other sources.

You will be required to remit quarterly tax instalments to the Canada Revenue Agency if the net tax owing is more than $3,000 in the current year and in either of the two previous years ($1,800 in the province of Quebec). You can order CRA handout P110 on Paying Your Income Tax by Instalments for a discussion of your options.

Deductions (such as RRSP contributions and Carrying Charges) allow us to reduce the amount of income that is subject to taxation; credits reduce the amount of tax paid, tax-sheltered vehicles generally defer taxes to the future. You may now become eligible to claim credits and deductions you didn't have the opportunity to claim during your working life. It's time to take a tax refresher.

In the area of tax planning, it is important to get qualified advice on your situation. What follows is a general guide and some of these topics are covered in more detail elsewhere in the text. Current information is available on the CRA web site at (cra.gc.ca) and you may find (taxtips.ca) another helpful resource.

Tax Credits

Age Amount

Taxpayers aged 65 and over at the end of the year are eligible for this credit (federal credit of $6,408[1] for 2009) provided their net income is below a threshold amount (there are provincial *and* federal thresholds).

1. This amount reflects the January 27, 2009 Federal Budget. Check the CRA web site.

Tax Strategies in Retirement

Check the CRA web site (cra.gc.ca) for current levels. The federal credit begins to be clawed back at incomes over $32,312 and is completely lost at incomes over $75,032. This should increase your interest in effective income-splitting strategies.

Pension Income Amount

This is a federal tax credit (provincial credits may also apply) of up to $2,000 that applies to eligible pension income which at age 65 and over includes employer pension payments, annuity payments from registered funds and payments from RRIFs, LIFs, and LRIFs. Under age 65, only employer pension-plan payments qualify unless other eligible payments are received because of the death of the partner or spouse. See notes under Income Splitting.

Disability Credit

If a qualified person (usually a medical doctor) certifies that you have a severe and prolonged mental or physical impairment that markedly restricts your ability to perform certain defined basic activities of daily living, then a disability amount may be claimed. CRA form T2201, Disability Tax Credit Certificate must be completed and filed. There are federal and provincial credits. Caregiver Tax Credits may also be relevant while providing care to a dependant adult (not a spouse) residing in your home.

Medical Expenses

This tax credit is not only available for retired persons but you may have found yourself ineligible for the deduction during your working life because your income was too high or the share of medical expenses paid from your own pocket was too low. Chances are this tax credit will become more important as older taxpayers tend to incur more eligible expenses and have less third-party coverage.

Eligible expenses include bathroom aids such as hand rails, mobility aids such as wheelchairs, scooters and walkers, vision and hearing aids, homecare services and dentures to name a few. Should you claim medical expenses for full-time care in a nursing home, you may be ineligible to claim the disability amount.

Details are available on the CRA website (cra.gc.ca) and Interpretation Bulletin IT519R2 Consolidated, Medical Expense and Disability Tax Credits and Attendant Care Expense Deduction may be useful. Don't forget premiums for private health coverage including healthcare coverage while travelling!

The lower-income spouse can claim eligible medical expenses for both partners and can choose any 12-month period ending in the tax year in order to maximize the expenses. The federal tax credit is for medical expenses incurred over and above a threshold amount for 2009 of $2,011 or 3% of net income, whichever is lower.

Charitable Donations

Donations can be claimed by either spouse but it is more tax effective if the higher-income earner claims all contributions. The federal credit is calculated at the lowest marginal rate for the first $200 and 29% on any amount over that (plus provincial credits). You can carry the contributions forward for five years to earn a bigger credit.

Tuition, Education and Textbook Credits

Many of us will contemplate a return to school in retirement. Fees must be a minimum of $100 per course and the institution must issue either a T2202 or T2202A. Federal credits may be available for full- or part-time studies and students may qualify to claim tuition and education expenses incurred outside Canada! See the CRA's web site for further details.

Tax Deductions

Moving Expenses

Students who move away to attend post-secondary education and then move back to take employment or those who move more than 40km for a job may be able to claim some of their costs at tax time. If you are contemplating a move in retirement, look into it! Maybe you will take a job at Home Depot while you renovate that new retirement home you just moved to.

Carrying Charges and Investment Costs

Be sure to track fees for safety deposit boxes, borrowing costs for non-sheltered investments, investment counselling fees (not brokerage fees) and accounting fees (not tax returns). Administration fees for registered accounts (RRIFs, LIFs) and the new TFSAs are not eligible.

Eligible Business Expenses

If you have been an employee throughout your primary career, you are well aware that eligible deductions from your income are few are far between. Businesses and the self-employed have more opportunities to reduce taxable income.

If we work from home, we have the ability to deduct a portion of home-related expenses such as a share of the utilities, insurance and maintenance costs. The size of the home office determines the amount that can be deducted. If the office occupies 15% of the home, 15% of the operating expenses are deductible from income. If the business is unincorporated, the home-office expenses cannot be used to create a loss but they can be carried forward to deduct against future income.

Business owners can deduct any reasonable expenses they incur to earn business income. In my case, an Internet connection and newspaper subscriptions to financial and related topics are necessary for me to stay current in my field. Office supplies, legal and accounting costs, fees for professional memberships and 50% of the cost of business related entertaining are all deductible. Automobile expenses related to business use of a vehicle are also eligible. *Reasonable* salaries paid to spouses and other family members for legitimate contributions to business operations are deductible and provide another avenue for income splitting. The CRA has a number of publications for further details.

Tax Shelters

Tax Free Savings Accounts

As of January 2009, a new tax-saving option was created. These accounts are covered under Personal Investments. They are very valuable for all retirees to shelter investment income from tax (they don't simply defer the tax) and for partners to income split. Be sure to learn about them.

RRSPs and Spousal Retirement Savings Plans

These accounts are covered under Personal Investments and Income Splitting, below. Provided you have earned income (rental income from investment properties and employment or self-employment counts, investment earnings from your portfolio does not) you can continue to contribute to registered accounts until you turn 71! It is possible to continue to contribute to a spousal account after you are 71 provided the spouse is under 71.

Registered Disability Savings Plans (RDSPs)

This program was announced in March 2007 but financial institutions have been slow to make the accounts available. The first accounts just came on stream in early 2009. These accounts allow the plan holder to save up to $200,000 in a tax-deferred account on behalf of a disabled beneficiary age 59 or younger who qualifies for the disability tax credit.

Generous government assistance is available via an income-matching grant program and bond incentive programs that are income-tested. If you have a disabled family member you want to provide for, you simply *must* look into this program. See hrsdc.gc.ca under RDSPs.

Registered Education Savings Plans (RESPs)

My mother gave a very special gift to her all grandchildren by contributing to their education costs through a family RESP account. I want to do the same for my grandchildren one day but I just need to get some first! An RESP is a tax-sheltered fund to be used for the benefit of the named beneficiary (or beneficiaries) for post-secondary education. You can name yourself as a beneficiary. Non-tax-deductible contributions may be made annually or as a lump sum to a total maximum value of $50,000 per beneficiary. Earnings are sheltered until withdrawn and are then taxed at the student's presumably lower tax bracket. We can contribute to these plans for 31 years and they can remain open for 35 years. Best of all is a generous "free lunch" in the form of a 20% Canada Education Savings Grant (CESG) that provides a maximum $500 per year for a $2,500 contribution each year until the beneficiary turns 17. There are additional amounts available for low- to mid-income families and from some provinces.

It is my plan to contribute to an RESP in the plan's early years when my adult children will have many competing financial priorities (RRSP contributions and mortgage payments). I'll stop when I've reached the limit of the resources I'm prepared to commit and allow them to open their own plans for their kids. Further details on the program can be found on the CRA web site.

Income-Splitting Opportunities

We have already covered RESPs, RDSPs and paying salaries from your business as options to income split with family members. Some ways to share income with your spouse or partner are covered later in this chapter. This section is devoted to income splitting with other family members.

Give It to the "Kids"

As a parent or grandparent, you may wish to give cash for investments to your children or grandchildren. With gifts to a child under the age of majority, interest income or dividends earned on that gift will attribute back to *you* for income tax purposes. It will not attribute back to you if the minor child earns capital gains on that money. Note here that we cannot give cash to a spouse either – that too will be subject to income attribution.

If we give money to *adult* children, the CRA presumes we will not benefit financially from the gift and the earned investment income is not attributed back to the giver. They correctly assume we won't be seeing *that* money again! Those who choose to "protect" their adult children's financial interests should they take up with the proverbial "ne'er-do-well" or "gold digger" may wish to structure gifts as loans instead, either with an interest charge (we must claim and pay tax on this income) or as an interest-free loan. Should a relationship unravel, the loan will be called back. Legal advice will be prudent.

If you choose to give assets rather than cash, capital gain issues may arise. Assets are gifted at fair market value and gains dealt with on your tax return at the time of the gift. You cannot give the family cottage/cabin to your adult children unless you are prepared to pay the tax on any capital gain, that gain being the difference between what you paid for the place and its fair market value at the time of the gift.

Don't be in too big a hurry to give it away; you may need to conserve your resources to fund your own retirement.

Trusts

Income splitting with family members is also possible by creating an *inter vivos* or living trust during your lifetime. Property transferred to the trust triggers a deemed disposition and gains or losses may result. This type of trust can be useful for small business owners as part of an estate freeze or as a means of assuring future gains in an asset such as the family cottage, which accrues to other family members. Trusts are sophisticated structures and legal and accounting advice should be obtained.

Income Splitting With a Spouse or Partner

As we move into our retirement life phase, two financial issues for couples become quite important. How do we share the income we receive in order to pay the lowest tax rates? How do we assure our continued eligibility for means-tested programs such as Old Age Security or tax credits such as the Age Credit?

Look at the tax chart in Life Design and Planning. The chart shows that a couple will pay taxes at lower rates if each has a retirement income of $30,000 rather than all $60,000 being taxed in the same hands. As retirement approaches, an assessment of the future retirement income that will come into each persons hands is important.

Method #1 – Split Pension Income

For tax years 2007 and forward, the Federal Government allowed couples receiving *eligible pension income* to split *up to 50%* of that income when filing their returns. What qualifies as eligible pension income?

Those *age 65 or over* are eligible to split the following sources of income:

1. Registered Pension Plan payments (Company Defined Benefit Plans)
2. RRIF Payments (including LIFs and LRIFs created through Defined Contribution Pensions)

3. Lifetime annuities purchased from Registered funds (RRSPs)
4. The interest component only of Prescribed and non-Prescribed annuities

Those *under age 65*
1. Registered Pension Plan payments (Defined Benefit Plans)
2. Funds from 2 to 4 above only if received because of the death of a spouse

So what is *ineligible* for income splitting? Old Age Security (OAS), Guaranteed Income Supplement (GIS), RRSP withdrawals (I must have a RIF and be 65 and over) and income from Retirement Compensation Agreements (RCAs). Technically, Canada Pension Plan (CPP or QPP) is also ineligible but an opportunity for splitting this income already exists under separate legislation provided we are both over 60 years of age (refer to the section on Government Benefits). You cannot split investment income such as dividends, interest income, capital gains or rental income from investment properties if those investments are owned in *your name only*.

If you are prepared to wait until age 65 to retire *and* if most of your income will be from pensions or RRIFs, or from investments held in joint accounts, the restrictions on income splitting won't seriously affect you. Many of my clients retired in their late 50s and early 60s. If it is your intention to retire early, you need to pave the way for future income splitting in other ways.

Before you automatically split all eligible pension income 50/50 with your spouse, use tax software or ask your accountant to model possible scenarios. OAS claw-back begins at a base amount of $66,335 (2009) and the claw-back amounts to 15% of the income over the base – it will be fully clawed back at a net income of approximately $107,000. Age and pension credits are also phased out at higher incomes. We don't want to transfer so much income that our spouse loses these valuable credits. Regretfully, many of us will not have the too-much-income problem.

Method #2 – Spousal RRSP Accounts

Spousal RRSPs continue to be one of the most effective strategies for income splitting; particularly if you plan to retire before age 65. The change in income splitting legislation doesn't change the value of the spousal RRSP.

As covered previously, RRSP contribution room is calculated each year at 18% of previous year's earned income minus my PA (Pension Adjustment) to a maximum of $21,000 (2009). Ex. 18% of $50,000 – $ 0 PA = $9000 RRSP Contribution Room.

The contributor has the choice of contributing this amount to his or her own RRSP or to an RRSP in the spouse's name – called a spousal RRSP, or making a split between the accounts. The contributor (usually the highest-income earner) will claim the deduction on his or her income tax return but ultimately the withdrawal will be taxed in the spousal account holder's hands.

Caution! If the spouse withdraws the funds within three years of the most recent contribution, it will attribute back to the contributor for tax. Revenue Canada views this as "last money in, first money out."

Method #3 – Gift a TFSA Contribution

High-income earners can give the $5,000 TFSA contribution to a lower or no-income spouse or partner with no income attribution.

Future investment earnings are earned in the lower-income spouse's name and never taxed.

Method #4 - Share or Shift Investment Income

The Canada Revenue Agency says if I earned *all* the money that makes up a taxable investment account then I must pay the tax on 100% of the investment earnings from the account – *even if I hold these investments in a joint account!* To the CRA, the important issue is whose pockets the investment funds originated from. If we both contributed 50% of the investment dollars through our regular savings, we can split the investment income and tax burden 50/50. If I contributed 25% then the tax split on income will be 25/75.

Shift

To comply with this tax ruling, the higher-paying spouse can pay all the household bills and the lower-paid spouse can concentrate on the savings. That would create an investment pot in the lower-income earner's name; dividends, capital gains or interest income earned on these investments will be taxed in his or her hands.

Loan

If I *give* my spouse $100,000 to invest, 100% of the investment returns are attributed back to me for tax purposes. My alternative is to set up a formal loan agreement, charging my spouse Canada Revenue Agency's prescribed loan rate (changes announced quarterly, see CRA site). Provided my spouse pays the required interest each year (which I must claim as investment income), any investment returns will be taxed in my spouse's name.

These are somewhat complicated arrangements but, over time, they can shift income into the lower- or no-income spouse's name. The second-generation returns will be taxed in the spouse's hands.

Inheritance

If the lower-income spouse receives an inheritance and invests the funds in his or her name only, all investment income will be taxed in his or her hands. Some legal issues should be considered in this circumstance.

Retirement Tax Strategy Summary

Below is a summary of the key areas to consider for minimizing taxation and thereby increasing cash flow in retirement.

Tax Credits

Age amount and/or pension income amount
Medical expenses and charitable donations
Tuition, education and textbook credits
Disability credit

Tax Deductions

Moving expenses and/or eligible business expenses
Carrying charges and investment costs

Tax Shelters

Tax-Free Savings Accounts (TFSA)
RRSPs and Spousal Retirement Savings Plan
Registered Disability Savings Plans (RDSPs)
Registered Education Savings Plans (RESPs)

Income Splitting Opportunities

Giving it away to the "kids"

Splitting income with spouse or partner, spousal RRSPs

Giving a TFSA contribution

Sharing or shifting investment income, shift, loan, trusts

To do:
* Develop an investment policy statement
* Review asset mix, geographic distribution
* Examine the tax efficiency of your portfolio

Finances

Estate Planning and Life Insurance

It is very certain that the
desire of life prolongs it.

Lord Byron

Estate Planning and Life Insurance

Dealing with estate planning and life insurance issues is important throughout our life but becomes ever more important as we inch closer to the departure lounge.

An estate planning review includes assessing the financial needs of our survivors and reviewing our life insurance coverage and key documents. A key document review should include regularly reviewing the terms of your Will, Powers of Attorney for Property and Personal Care and beneficiary designations made on property not dealt with by the will.

Life Insurance

Life insurance was crucial when we had a young family, just one household breadwinner and large debts. At your present stage, the question needs to be asked if you STILL need life insurance. The first step is to consider if you are "hit by a truck." Are there sufficient assets to feed, water, educate, and take care of everyone you love and feel the need to take care of? If the pot isn't large enough, then you need life insurance to fund the difference. It is my *personal* view that as we gradually build our net worth, and children leave the nest and become self-supporting, our need for life insurance coverage declines.

My two boys are close to being off the payroll. There is enough to feed, water and educate them, and see them independently launched. What about Dennis? Is there enough in that pot to look after Dennis for the balance of his lifetime in the manner to which *I* think he should be accustomed? Well I won't be funding any dancing retinue for him but I believe he'll be just fine. We have no debts I need to clear and my estate should be able to honour any charitable bequests I choose to make from the remaining assets. All of this is true for *today* but each time I review, I will ask the same questions. My personal conclusion is that I don't need to maintain much life insurance.

The key to that conclusion is that it is not my intention to leave a large estate to *adult* children. I raised my boys as a single parent and feel I paid my dues having the sole responsibility of feeding, watering, educating and launching them. However, there are clearly two camps on this issue. My camp says, "Kids, I'm going to work really hard throughout my retirement to spend every dime I have. If I miss the mark and can't spend it all, you can have what's left."

For a number of the individuals I advised, leaving an estate was *very* important and they often had a specific number associated with that objective. Some wanted to leave each adult child $10,000; some wanted to leave each half a million dollars. The number would vary but the intent was the same – to leave an estate. For those wanting to leave an estate, they either had to have deep enough pockets that they couldn't spend it all, deny themselves a better lifestyle to avoid spending it all, or use life insurance as an option to fund the legacy.

The next task is to consider which type of insurance to purchase: term life insurance, whole life insurance, universal life insurance, or variable life insurance. You need a professional to help you evaluate the merits of these options but as a good Scot with some insurance training, I have a bias toward term insurance. For many, it provides the best "bang for the buck" and doesn't co-mingle investment with insurance objectives, but I readily acknowledge it is *not* the solution for every situation or every estate plan.

The Wizard of Id is one of my favourite comic strips. In one strip, we see a life insurance salesman approaching a farmer saying, "Can I interest you in some life insurance?" The farmer replies, "I have too much now." "What constitutes too much?" inquires the salesman. "I'm afraid to go to sleep before *she* does," says the farmer while pointing to his wife. If that's your situation, perhaps you do have too much life insurance!

If you still have large outstanding debts, you need to consider insurance. If you have minor children and insufficient assets to see them to independence, you need to consider insurance. If you are the sole breadwinner and you would prefer your homemaking spouse remain at home, you may need insurance.

Some of us have ambitious charitable aims to leave a legacy to the organizations that are important to us. Insurance is one way to make that possible. You may have assets that will attract a great deal of capital gains tax on your passing, such as family cottages or businesses and choose to cover the ensuing tax tab through insurance.

One of my clients owned an expensive lake property. When he purchased that property it didn't cost much, but now the property is worth over a million dollars. The property was jointly held and on his death, it could pass tax-free to his surviving spouse. On her death, capital gains tax would be due. Tax was payable on half of the difference between fair market value and the adjusted cost base of the cottage/cabin at her tax rate. The tax tab was sizeable; probate fees could also be sizeable depending on the province. It was his objective that the asset remain in the family rather than being sold to pay the tax bill so he insured that result with a joint last-to-die life insurance policy.

He had his adult children pay the insurance premiums because they were ultimately the beneficiaries of a valuable asset. There are other methods to pass on the family cottage and reduce the taxes owing with proper planning. Pay to get good advice.

For many, the decision to retire will have an effect on their insurance coverage through the loss of company insurance plans. Be sure to review these issues.

Mortgage Insurance

I'm not a big fan of mortgage life insurance. Many of my clients have found that mortgage insurance through the bank can often be more expensive than a term policy taken out directly with a life insurance company. Of course, the bank has the decided advantage of convenience.

If you take mortgage insurance from the bank for your outstanding mortgage of $100,000, they will charge a premium based on $100,000 of coverage. You are paying that mortgage down over time. If you pass away and the mortgage has been reduced to

$60,000, the mortgage insurance will cover only the outstanding mortgage balance. If you had an outside insurance policy, it would pay your estate $100,000. I like that math better but be sure to put the insurance in place!

Planning for the Exit Ramp

Any planning for the rest of your life must also consider your death. A clear plan is necessary for the exit ramp! It's tricky to discuss estate planning in a book intended for all Canadians, because estate legislation is provincially regulated. Keep this in mind should you make a decision to retire to a province (or country) other than the one your will was drafted in! This discussion is intended to get you thinking about these issues, but please seek knowledgeable, professional assistance. I tease attendees in my retirement seminars that my accounting and legal comments are worth the amount they are paying me directly for them – nothing, zero!

We can distribute our assets in a number of ways both before and after our death. On our death, a will describes our final wishes but we can also distribute assets through gifts while we are alive or through trusts. Assets can pass to beneficiaries outside of our will or estate and in that way may avoid probate.

Intestate

If you die not having made a will, you are said to have died "intestate." If you don't have a formal will, Provincial Intestate Succession Acts will dictate how your assets are distributed and this may not be in keeping with your wishes. A spouse inherits 100% if there are no children (Quebec 1/3 spouse, 1/3 parents, 1/3 siblings). If there are children, the spouse receives only the "preferential" amount (a minimum amount which varies by province), and then shares the balance with the children.

Rules apply in the absence of a spouse or children and benefit first parents, then siblings, and so on. If no relatives remain, the government receives the estate. An application must be made to the court to appoint an estate Administrator. Once appointed, the Administrator must act in ways outlined by the Court. Estate property; investments may be liquidated with no attention to appropriate timing. Potential guardians must apply to the Court to assume custody of your children. Not having a valid will should not be an option for anyone!

Wills

Some jurisdictions will accept as valid a will in our own handwriting. This is called a "holographic will." Our tech-savvy kids think they can tap this will out on their computer and print it off. That's not a valid holographic will. It must be in your *own handwriting*. While witnesses are not required, some jurisdictions will require it to be signed. This is an unsophisticated will open to misinterpretation and our affairs would need to be straightforward for this to do the job. I certainly don't recommend it.

I'm not a fan of "will-kits" either. Typically, they are the "will-kit for Canadians" and our legislation is province-specific. Often the intent of statements made in these documents is not clear. A will-kit can, however, provide a useful outline to guide your discussion ahead of an appointment with a lawyer. If we are going to arm wrestle over who the "alternate executor" should be, let's do it at home and not on billable time!

A will prepared by a lawyer might run to $500 for most couples with an uncomplicated estate. A more complicated estate could certainly cost $2,000 or more, but for most of us that's a small price to pay to ensure our assets are distributed as we'd like. I also want a lawyer with estate expertise, not the lawyer I used for my last real estate transaction!

If you get married, your will becomes void, but a will is not voided by divorce. A will must be signed in front of two witnesses who are not beneficiaries under the will. A will should be reviewed every five years or less or any time there's a change in circumstances. A change in circumstances includes a move to another province or country, children reaching adulthood and no longer needing a guardian, the birth or death of an heir, the sale of a business or other asset referred to in the will or tax law changes. I have met 80-year-olds who didn't have a will; talk about false optimism! I have also seen clients at 90 who still had guardians named for their 70-year-old children. Dust off that will!

Executor

Picking an executor is a key issue. The executor is our personal representative and s/he has a long laundry list of duties, including locating, valuing and distributing our assets as we have directed. S/he will also cancel credit cards, subscriptions, utilities, healthcare cards and notify the government. We can appoint one or more persons or appoint a trust company. Often one spouse will name the other but we need another choice should they die together and a second alternate is named in the event the first declines the role or dies first. Our executor must live in our country and it is best that s/he lives in our province.

Perhaps there's no family member whom you think is mature or knowledgeable enough to take on this role. An advantage of corporate executorships is that they will bring the expertise necessary to do the job well. However, the corporate executor, or any executor for that matter, is entitled to charge a fee for this service.

Guardian

Another key role is that of guardian for our children under the age of majority. This person will feed, water, and educate the kids in our absence. This is quite a different skill set than we ask for from the executor. Spouses will typically name each other, but in the absence of both parents, who shall we name? We need a first and second alternate. As the years pass, make sure you feel your original choice is still up to the job!

Trustee

The third role is that of trustee. This person manages our financial assets until beneficiaries are entitled to receive them. The executor is commonly named as the trustee. Children cannot inherit assets until the age of majority or later if that is what you specify. Many 20-year-olds are not mature enough to handle a sizeable estate!

When we name someone for any of these jobs, whether it be executor, guardian, or trustee, we need that person's permission first. We are asking them to take on a serious responsibility and a time-consuming obligation. We want to be sure they are of a mind to do that. In order for your executor to pay outstanding debt obligations, cancel credit cards etc. and manage your assets until disbursement, *you* need to stay financially current. Always maintain a current Net Worth Statement.

In my experience with clients, I found most beneficiaries (adult children) didn't really have a problem with the way mom and dad decided to divide the financial assets. The real issues occurred with the "stuff" and making decisions over which one got the birthday plate or grandma's silver chest. We can write a separate informal memorandum to be given to our executor that describes the disposition of personal property. It is simpler to revise this than to draft a codicil to the will if the birthday plate is broken! My mother has the endearing habit of putting labels on the back of the artwork on her wall and changing those labels from time to time. You might find us curiously peeking at the labels when we are visiting!

Probate

Probate is a legal or judicial procedure where your will is verified and the appointment and authority of your executor to act is confirmed by the courts under provincial legislation. Outside parties such as banks, trust companies and all manner of financial services firms and land titles registries can and will refuse to transfer the deceased's assets to the named beneficiaries without the legal comfort and assurance of a grant of probate or probated will.

Filing fees are charged by the court to issue the grant of probate and these fees range from negligible in some provinces to *considerable* in others, leading some to look for ways to "avoid probate." Some jurisdictions cap fees at amounts ranging from $140 to $400 so check first whether the fee in your province warrants some special planning.

Some estate-planning techniques will reduce the value of the assets flowing through the estate and therefore reduce the fees but look into competent advice rather than "home handyman" solutions!

Power of Attorney for Property

A POA for property assigns authority to someone else to take over our financial affairs. As the donor, we decide the range of powers we are assigning. These can be temporary while we are out of the country or can cover specific issues such as banking or real estate or a general POA that allows broad powers. Typically, the authority terminates if the donor becomes mentally incompetent; on death, it terminates with the will coming into play.

To survive incompetency, an Enduring POA is required. A POA can be designated as a springing POA, meaning it becomes effective only in the event of the donor's incapacity; the document should describe how incapacity is to be proved.

My 92-year-old mother has named two of us as co-attorneys with quite broad-ranging powers; however, we can act only when two doctors agree she has lost her marbles!

The husband of one of my clients was mentally incapacitated by a serious stroke. She was unable to care for him at home and needed to sell the family home to access sufficient resources to afford his care. In some jurisdictions, a spouse is unable to sell or mortgage a matrimonial home even if it is jointly held. She had a costly and time-consuming application to the courts for a trusteeship order under the Dependant Adult's Act. The problem could have been avoided with an Enduring Power of Attorney (EPA).

In some provinces, an EPA can deal only with financial responsibilities and not healthcare issues. Dealing with healthcare responsibilities is an increasingly important issue.

Power of Attorney for Personal Care

In some provinces, a POA or EPA can assign authority to another for non-financial decisions. In other provinces, a Personal Directive, Healthcare Directive or living will must exist. We create these documents while we are still physically and mentally able in order to define the extremes of care we would want healthcare professionals to go to if we couldn't make decisions. Where allowed, we would name the individual responsible for making decisions.

Do we want to be maintained on a respirator or fed via a feeding tube? Does the person named have the authority to select our care facility? Check the requirements in your province.

With a smile, I suggest to clients they might want the medical care decisions in separate hands from the financial responsibility! Dennis tells me he would never want to make the difficult decision to "turn the tap off" for me so I have named another family member who would make the difficult decisions. A copy of this directive should be in the hands of the attorney, close family members and doctors.

Trusts

Trusts are complicated and you should have both legal and accounting advice to set one up. We can distribute our assets through "Living Trusts" or "Testamentary Trusts."

It is not uncommon in second marriages to see a form of testamentary trust called a spousal trust that gives the surviving spouse income for their lifetime but on their passing, the capital passes back to the adult children of the first marriage.

Trusts can also be established to hold assets until children are older, to protect spendthrift beneficiaries, for the benefit of mentally or physically disabled beneficiaries, or to realize tax savings.

Gifts

If we are in a hurry to give it away, we can give gifts while we are alive! Remember from our chapter on taxation that there may be income attribution and/or capital gains considerations.

Outside the Will

Naming a beneficiary directly on life insurance policies, RRSPs or Pension Plans means the assets will pass to the beneficiary outside the will or estate and will not be subject to probate fees. The tax-free rollover on sheltered assets is available only to the spouse/common-law partner, dependant minor or dependant disabled child.

Announced in the January 2009 budget, the government has changed the way RRSP and RRIF values are determined on death when passing to other, non-rollover beneficiaries. Previously, the fair market value would be determined just prior to death and included as taxable income in a final tax return. If the account fell in value prior to distribution, the estate still paid taxes based on the higher value at death. The recent budget allows the lesser value to be deducted from the initial valuation in a final return for payouts after January 1, 2009.

Assets held as joint tenants with right of survivorship (JTWROS) such as your home or joint bank accounts allows assets to pass outside the estate and avoid probate; however there may be other issues with joint accounts. Be aware of the difference between joint tenants and tenants in common. While both designations allow an equal share in the rights and income of the property, on death the interest of a tenant in common passes to his or her beneficiary, not to the other tenant in common.

It is common for elderly clients whose spouse has passed away to hold assets jointly with one or more adult children for estate planning purposes. Recent court cases have created a distinction between legal and beneficial ownership. Be sure to gain an understanding of the terms and document your intentions at the time of the transfer of the assets or you may create unintended tax and probate consequences. Legal ownership presumes the adult child is holding the asset for the benefit of the estate – there is no deemed disposition or tax on the transfer, and probate fees will apply. Under beneficial ownership there *is* a deemed disposition and subsequent gain or loss consequences plus sharing of future income for tax purposes. In this instance, probate fees will *not* apply.

Exiting the Departure Lounge

On our passing, our family and/or our executor needs to know where key documents are, where we keep our tax files, who our lawyer and accountant is, where we keep instructions for our burial and whether there are pre-paid funeral plans and so on. Communicate to others where this information can be located.

For those who wish to make funeral preferences clear, contact the Memorial Society Association of Canada. They have a web site that identifies contacts across the country. Upon payment of a modest membership fee, they will send you an information package that includes a "statement for the guidance of my survivors upon my death" and they pre-negotiate cost-conscious funeral plans with funeral homes across the country that you have an option to prepay, or not. We can also make our arrangements directly with funeral homes.

None of us relishes making these arrangements or contemplating our own demise but we make life easier for our survivors if they have some direction in this regard.

One of my clients kept very up-to-date information. Our only challenge was that he kept it password protected on his computer. That's not useful! Make a habit of regularly burning a new CD with current information. On the back of the CD, note the password and tuck the CD, the keys to the safety deposit box and perhaps a copy of the will and funeral instructions in a readily identifiable location that you have made others aware of. Then get on with the business of living!

To do: * Review life insurance requirements
               * Review and update the will
               * Draft or review POA or EPA (for health and property)

Conclusion

Nurture your relationships. Develop a lifestyle that is healthy and exciting. Manage your finances well. Your retirement will ROCK!

Making a Difference
About the Authors

LIFESTYLE | RELATIONSHIP | FINANCES

Conclusion

Making a Difference

*A life is not important except in
the impact it has on other lives.*

Jackie Robinson

*Each person must live their
life as a model for others.*

Rosa Parks

Making a Difference

What will your legacy be? What do you want your epitaph to say?
How would you like to be remembered by those who walked beside
you or followed behind you? What kind of an effect on others and
on the world do you desire and strive for? What do you do and how
do you act each day to make your mark? How will those who follow
know that you were here?

Brownie F., a wife, mother, grandmother, great-grandmother, friend,
nurse and inspiration passed away in Winnipeg in 2008. In a recent
tribute in the Globe and Mail, her family said, "Brownie had a long
and terrific run, inspiring family and friends with her positive

attitude, her intelligence and her amazing zest for life." I didn't know Brownie but I wish I had!

Most of us would describe ourselves as everyday, ordinary people. The heroes and mentors are those we remember most and those who influenced our life most profoundly. They would describe themselves the same way – as everyday people.

What allows ordinary people to have an extraordinary influence on others? Perhaps it's this rule: when we remember what matters most to us, our ability to make a difference is at its most powerful.

Donor Alvin Grunert gave $1.5 million to Thompson Rivers University in Kamloops as a memorial tribute to his wife. He grew up on a farm in Saskatchewan and never went beyond grade 8. He then spent 30 years working as a prison guard. He earned the money through shrewd investments in the market and felt he had more than he needed. He gave this challenge to the guests at a university event to honour his gift: "If I can step up here and change the world tonight, what will you do tomorrow?"

Rod and Ingrid Mc Carroll, a Calgary couple, spent time in Mexico in 2005 and 2006 introducing simple bio-sand water filters to Mexico's poor to give them access to clean drinking water. Ingrid said, "It's a pivotal point in your life, when you go from me-centered to people-centered."

We learned about Toothena, the Tooth Fairy, spreading healthy smiles in Kenya in the chapter on volunteering. We don't have to travel the world, however, because we can change the world from the comfort of our armchair! Better the World, which describes itself as a for-profit social venture has launched a "surf for charity" program powered by Google.

Invest in Making a Difference

Some boomers will create a lasting legacy through building a business that carries on after their passing, others by contributing to or creating a charitable foundation. Some will do it through their loving presence and life wisdom shared with their community or simply with their family.

What gifts would you share with the world if you knew it was your last chance? Randy Pausch, a young professor at Carnegie Mellon, passed away from pancreatic cancer in July 2008, leaving behind a wife and three young children. Many of you already know the story of Randy; an *extraordinary*, ordinary man who became an Internet sensation when his *"Last Lecture"* was watched by millions on You Tube. His follow-up book has been equally successful (thelastlecture.com). He lectured about the joy of life, the important values of integrity and gratitude and other things he held as crucial for a rich and meaningful life.

He knew the end of his lecture had to be a distillation of how he felt about the end of his life. He told attendees that his lecture, titled "Really Achieving Your Childhood Dreams," contained two "head fakes." First, it wasn't about how to achieve your dreams but "it's about how to lead your life. If you lead your life the right way, the karma will take care of itself." His second head fake was that the lecture wasn't really meant for those in attendance but "it was for my kids." What a wonderful legacy he left them and all of us. Live well, contribute to the world and to your family where and how you can.

The example of *your* life well lived is the best and most powerful legacy of all. Our wish for you is a rich and juicy retirement life. Live large and make the changes you need to in your life to help you live that bigger life. Take some risks, develop a can-do attitude, let go of the small stuff, be authentic and know yourself physically, emotionally and spiritually. Be open to receive the pleasures and fulfillment of a big life. *Let your Retirement Rock!*

A quote we love says it best:

"I don't want to get to the end of my life and find that I just lived the length of it. I want to have lived the width of my life as well."

Diane Acromyn

About the Authors

Heather and Dennis met in 1995; they were married in 2000. They view their relationship as a committed life partnership. Both chose to leave their long-time careers in 2004, Heather at age 50 and Dennis at age 54. Together they have four adult children.

Heather Compton enjoyed a long and successful career as a stockbroker and financial advisor, retiring as a vice president with a major bank-owned financial firm. She continues to be involved in her profession as a presenter and facilitator of pre-retirement planning seminars, and now as an author.

Dennis Blas retired after a 35-year career in Information Technology, the last 20 years working in management roles with large petroleum and transportation companies. In a volunteer capacity over a 10-year period, he facilitated group programs providing education and support to those experiencing major life transitions.

The authors are enjoying their retirement together. They share their experiences as a retired couple and those of others who have crossed their paths. One of their most valuable messages has not to do with money, nor work, but with relationship. They have discovered that ongoing relationship re-assessment, renewal and growth is fundamental to happiness, and that being "retired" provides countless opportunities to make that a reality. Their retirement ROCKS!

Life Design and Planning

My Outlook and Vision
My Life List
My Lifestyle
My Relationships
My Finances

LIFESTYLE | RELATIONSHIP | FINANCES

Life Design and Planning

tools available from -
www.retirementrocks.ca

	.pdf file	EXCEL model
My Outlook and Vision	√	
My Life List	√	
My Lifestyle		
Gauging My Lifestyle	√	
Health Comes First	√	
Work and Volunteering	√	
Activities and Hobbies	√	
Travel Plans	√	
Housing / Lifestyle Priorities	√	
My Relationships	√	
My Finances		
How Much Measures	√	
How Much Forecaster	√	√
Net Worth Statement	√	√
Cash Flow Statement	√	√
Retirement Checklist	√	
Financial Appendix		
Future Value Tables	√	

My Outlook and Vision

www.retirementrocks.ca
for .pdf copy

Underline or write in the word(s) that best describe your present view of retirement.

Boring	Freedom	Stress free	Restful
Active	Frightening	Lonely	Exciting
Relaxing	Renewal	Possibility	Scarcity
....	....	....	....
....	....	....	....

Models of Retirement

Who do you know that has retired?
What have you learned from them as models of retirement?

Who?	**What I have learned from them**
1.	....
2.	....
3.	....

My Big Rocks!

List your life cornerstones (Big Rocks) in their order of importance.
Examples: health, relationships, work, activities, spirituality, finances

1.	4. ....
2.	5. ....
3.	6. ....

My Life List   www.retirementrocks.ca
for .pdf copy

Write down several new things you would like to accomplish or experience in your life. Think and dream as big as possible.

What do you want to do, feel, taste, smell, experience, or learn?
Where do you want to travel?

Wish, Dream, Experience, Accomplish   **by When?**

	Wish, Dream, Experience, Accomplish	by When?
1		
2		
3		
4		
5		
6		
7		
8		
9		
10		
11		
12		
13		
14		
15		
16		

A wish remains only that when there is no plan to achieve it.
A wish becomes an obtainable goal once a plan is in place.

Life Design and Planning

My Lifestyle

Gauging My Lifestyle
Health Comes First
Work and Volunteering
Activities and Hobbies
Travel Plans
Housing / Lifestyle Priorities

LIFESTYLE | RELATIONSHIP | FINANCES

Gauging My Lifestyle

www.retirementrocks.ca for .pdf copy

Date: _____

**My
Reading (R)**

☐

(R) *Work*

0 ▶ I work very long hours on an ongoing basis,
and will do this until I retire; then I will stop.

0.5

1 ▶ I work too much at a job I don't particularly
like and I am beginning to think about change.

1.5

2 ▶ I work hard and usually enjoy my work, but
my work-life balance could be improved.

2.5

3 ▶ I love my work and it meets my basic needs,
but work does not dictate my life choices.

☐

(R) *Relationships*

0 ▶ I am estranged from some of my immediate
family members, and have no close friends.

0.5

1 ▶ My family and friend relationships are weak,
and not very supportive to me emotionally.

1.5

2 ▶ I have good and supportive family and friend
relationships, but I tend to take them for granted.

2.5

3 ▶ I have, nurture, and rely upon close relationships
with my family and with my friends.

Gauging My Lifestyle   www.retirementrocks.ca for .pdf copy

Date: _____

**My
Reading (R)**

(R)   *Health*   ☐

0 ▶ I am not physically or emotionally healthy,
and am not doing anything to improve that.
0.5

1 ▶ I feel fine, so I do not believe that I am unhealthy,
and mostly my head is in the sand.
1.5

2 ▶ I am relatively healthy and go for regular
check-ups, but I am not disciplined about it.
2.5

3 ▶ I am healthy and continually focus on maintaining
good physical and emotional health.

(R)   *Activities*   ☐

0 ▶ I do not have any activities in my life, and
have no idea as to what activities I want.
0.5

1 ▶ I have an activity or two that fill time, but
my level of enjoyment is low.
1.5

2 ▶ I have activities in my life that I like, but need
to find ways to spend more time at them.
2.5

3 ▶ I have activities in my life that suspend time,
and that are meaningful and fulfilling.

Gauging My Lifestyle

www.retirementrocks.ca for .pdf copy

Date: _____

My
Reading (R)

☐

(R) *Stress*

0 ▶ I am constantly stressed in most areas of my life, and do nothing to manage that stress.

0.5

1 ▶ I know that my levels of stress are frequently too high, but I really don't have a choice.

1.5

2 ▶ I am sometimes over-stressed and deal with it, but haven't dealt with underlying causes.

2.5

3 ▶ I experience normal levels of stress, and my stress-management approach works well.

☐

(R) *Diet*

0 ▶ I never watch my diet, and frequently eat foods that I know are not good for my health.

0.5

1 ▶ I watch my diet only when it is convenient, and does not require too much self-sacrifice.

1.5

2 ▶ I usually maintain a well-balanced diet, but occasionally I fall off the wagon.

2.5

3 ▶ I maintain a well-balanced diet on a daily basis, and review it regularly with my doctor.

Gauging My Lifestyle   www.retirementrocks.ca for .pdf copy

Date: _____   **My Reading (R)**

(R)   *Exercise*   ☐

0 ▶   I never exercise, I am in poor shape, and I am
not really motivated to do anything about it.
0.5

1 ▶   I exercise occasionally, and only when it is for
fun, which usually means I hurt afterwards.
1.5

2 ▶   I exercise often, but not as often as I need to,
because other areas of my life get in the way.
2.5

3 ▶   I exercise on a regular basis to manage
stress, and help maintain my physical health.

(R)   *Intellect*   ☐

0 ▶   I do nothing to challenge myself mentally,
and don't care to learn anything new.
0.5

1 ▶   I do not welcome mental challenge, but can
force myself to be up to the task if necessary.
1.5

2 ▶   I like and look for intellectual stimulation in
my work, but not so much outside of work.
2.5

3 ▶   I constantly challenge my mind, and am
always exploring new learning opportunities.

Gauging My Lifestyle   www.retirementrocks.ca for .pdf copy

Date: _____   **My**
                                      Reading (R)

(R)   *Attitude*   ☐

0 ▶   I am pessimistic by nature; I fear life changes,
          and I do not look forward to retirement.
0.5

1 ▶   I often look at life and life changes with
          my glass half empty, and don't get engaged.
1.5

2 ▶   I am optimistic most of the time, catching myself
          when I am not and adjusting my outlook.
2.5

3 ▶   I maintain a positive attitude about
          life and life changes, including retirement.

(R)   *Money*   ☐

0 ▶   I have no sizable investments or financial
          plans, and am not saving enough for my future.
0.5

1 ▶   I have intentions to plan my finances, and
          to save more, but haven't moved forward.
1.5

2 ▶   I have financial plans and investments that
          I am happy with, but need to review and update.
2.5

3 ▶   I have a solid financial plan in place, and am
          doing my utmost to invest for my retirement.

Total Reading (R): _____

Gauging My Lifestyle   www.retirementrocks.ca for .pdf copy

Date: _____

Shade in the boxes, from left to right, up to your total reading.

0	5	10	15	20	25	30

Total Reading

0

. **It is not too late for me to make**
. **some important new life choices.**
.

10

. **I have begun to change and**
. **to see healthy improvement.**
.

20

. **My lifestyle is nearing the point**
. **that I am striving to get to.**
.

30

. **My lifestyle is healthy and is**
. **exactly how I plan to keep it.**
.

Health Comes First

www.retirementrocks.ca for .pdf copy

In each aspect of healthy aging, indicate whether attention is needed. Where attention is not needed, indicate what you must do to keep it that way. Where it is needed, indicate what you must begin to do or stop doing.

Aspect of Healthy Aging	Needs Attention?	I am Going to…
Physical:		
Regular Check-ups	_____	_____
Regular Exercise	_____	_____
Alcohol & Smoking	_____	_____
Diet and Weight	_____	_____
Emotional:		
Emotional Outlets	_____	_____
Social Network	_____	_____
Leisure Activities	_____	_____
_____	_____	_____
Mental:		
Job / Work	_____	_____
New Learning	_____	_____
Challenging Self	_____	_____
_____	_____	_____
Spiritual:		
Community	_____	_____
Practice	_____	_____
_____	_____	_____

Work and Volunteering

Basic Needs Met by Work

1. Meaningful pursuits
2. Daily routine
3. Identity and status
4. Belonging / community

5. ....
6. ....
7. ....
8. ....

Areas of business that I might like
to create or pursue for WORK:

1. ....
2. ....
3. ....
4. ....
5. ....
6. ....

Volunteer opportunities I want to get
involved in or find out more about:

1. ....
2. ....
3. ....
4. ....
5. ....
6. ....

Activities and Hobbies   www.retirementrocks.ca for .pdf copy

Activities I enjoy doing now, or enjoyed doing in the past and want to start doing again (activity types are solo or alone, with a partner or friend, or as a group):

Activity	Type	When? How often? With whom?
1.	....	....
2.	....	....
3.	....	....
4.	....	....

Activities I want to try that require training and/or learning in preparation (activity types are solo or alone, with a partner or friend, or as a group):

Activity	Type	New skills or knowledge needed
1.	....	....
2.	....	....
3.	....	....
4.	....	....

Activities that I am not interested in and do not intend to try:

1.	3.	5. ....
2.	4.	6. ....

Hobbies I would like to try, do more of, or bring back into my life:

1. ....
2. ....
3. ....

Travel Plans

www.retirementrocks.ca for .pdf copy

The top five places I want to travel to are:

	Destination	What I want (do or see)	With Whom
1.	....	....	....
2.	....	....	....
3.	....	....	....
4.	....	....	....
5.	....	....	....

Example: Egypt — pyramids, and the Valley of the Kings — organized and guided tour

My physical capabilities / special needs / required training are:

	What it is	What is needed	When
1.	....	....	_____
2.	....	....	_____
3.	....	....	_____
4.	....	....	_____
5.	....	....	_____
6.	....	....	_____

Examples:
kayaking trip	paddling lessons	Summer 09
running 10k	get in shape	Spring 10

Travel Plans

www.retirementrocks.ca for .pdf copy

Consolidated Travel Plans

	Travel Destinations	Type of Travel	With Whom	When or How Often
1.				
2.				
3.				
4.				
5.				
6.				
7.				
8.				
9.				
10.				
11.				
12.				

Examples:

1.	Africa (safari)	adventure	group	Jan 2010
2.	Vancouver	visit relatives	my sister	Jun 2012
3.	Costa Rica	beach vacation	friends	Feb 2015
4.	Toronto	work related	alone	Sep 2013
5.	California	activity based	my partner	every yr.

Housing / Lifestyle Priorities

www.retirementrocks.ca
for .pdf copy

Consider the following factors, and determine how important they are. Change and delete from the list, and add to the list as necessary. If you find that many of these factors are very important, try ranking the highs in the right column.

Factor	Importance Low	Med	High	High Rank
Living arrangements ("lock and leave" or conventional home)				
Relatively low-cost living arrangements and lifestyle				
Where to live (the location, the climate, and the culture)				
Proximity to family members (parents, children, grandchildren)				
Proximity to close friends; ability to make new friends				
Healthcare and access to healthcare facilities and services				
Amenities and access to personal activity facilities				
Meaningful work, including part-time and volunteer work				
Extensive travel (ease of arrangements and airport access)				
Financial security and comfort (having "enough" money)				
Ability to be involved with and contribute to "community"				
Commonality of spirituality / religious beliefs and practices				

Life Design and Planning

My Relationships

Life Partner
Friends
Family

LIFESTYLE | RELATIONSHIP | FINANCES

My Relationships

www.retirementrocks.ca for .pdf copy

Life Partner

Qualities and behaviours I see and appreciate in my life partner:

1. ....   4. ....
2. ....   5. ....
3. ....   6. ....

Key areas we handle differently and these differences are valued:

1. ....   4. ....
2. ....   5. ....
3. ....   6. ....

My relationship expectations going into retirement:

1.   ....
2.   ....
3.   ....
4.   ....

Life tasks / responsibilities I prefer on my partner's list, not mine:

1. ....   4. ....
2. ....   5. ....
3. ....   6. ....

Life tasks / responsibilities I'm willing to take from my life partner:

1. ....   4. ....
2. ....   5. ....
3. ....   6. ....

My Relationships

www.retirementrocks.ca for .pdf copy

Life Partner

What life tasks or responsibilities can we agree should be farmed out?

1. ....   4. ....
2. ....   5. ....
3. ....   6. ....

What am I looking forward to doing together with my partner?

1. ....
2. ....
3. ....
4. ....
5. ....
6. ....

What am I looking forward to doing without my partner?

1. ....
2. ....
3. ....
4. ....
5. ....
6. ....

My Relationships

www.retirementrocks.ca for .pdf copy

Friends

Friends to grow old with:

1. ....   7. ....
2. ....   8. ....
3. ....   9. ....
4. ....   10. ....
5. ....   11. ....
6. ....   12. ....

Pleasant Friends	*Engaged* Friends	*Meaningful* Friends
....	....	....
....	....	....
....	....	....
....	....	....

I want to expand my circle of friends, and will start to do this by:

1. ....
2. ....
3. ....
4. ....
5. ....

My Relationships

www.retirementrocks.ca for .pdf copy

Family and Friends

Personal relationships that I want to invest more time and energy on:

Who	Why… and what I want
1.	....
2.	....
3.	....
4.	....

Relationship Picture

Write the names or initials of the people in your life somewhere inside or outside of your relationship square depending on how important and/or healthy your relationship with each of them is. The closer they are to "ME" in the square, the more important they are and/or the healthier the relationship. Notice those that you would like to position differently.

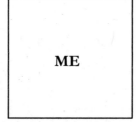

My Relationships

www.retirementrocks.ca for .pdf copy

Adult Children: My Personal Resolutions (my children):

   Who   **Resolution**

1. ....
2. ....
3. ....
4. ....

Adult Children: My Personal Resolutions (my step-children):

   Who   **Resolution**

1. ....
2. ....
3. ....
4. ....

Parents and In-laws: My Personal Resolutions:

   Who   **Resolution**

1. ....
2. ....
3. ....
4. ....

Life Design and Planning

My Finances

How Much is Enough Measures
How Much is Enough Forecaster
Net Worth Statement
Cash Flow Statement
Retirement Checklist

LIFESTYLE | RELATIONSHIP | FINANCES

How Much is "Enough" Measures

www.retirementrocks.ca
for .pdf copy

Enough money for me is ...

$ _____ per year, or

$ _____ per month, or

_____ % of my pre-retirement income.

I will know I have enough money when:

1. ....
2. ....
3. ....
4. ....
5. ....
6. ....
7. ....

Examples:

I can golf twice a week from May to September.

I can take one "big" trip every two or three years.

I can purchase a "new to me" car every few years.

I can host dinner parties for my friends and family.

How Much is Enough Forecaster

This worksheet determines a meaningful estimate of the amount of your spending and the size of your savings once you reach retirement. It also provides a "reasonableness" check.

Using Future Value (FV) Tables

The factors in the Future Value Tables represent the increased value of money over a number of years in the future (period) at a specific return on investment (ROI) %. Multiply the current or present value (today's value) of a sum of money by the factor located at the number of years in the future (period) and the expected ROI %.

There are two sets of tables provided. One set contains the factors applicable to each *existing* $1 in a fund invested over a period of time (use for existing lump sum savings). The other set contains the factors applicable to *adding* $1 *every year* to the existing fund over a period of time (use for annual contribution to savings).

Rate of Return, Inflation, and Tax

The calculated growth of an investment over time using an expected rate of return (ROI) is independent of inflation and taxes. In order to determine the real or net gain, inflation and taxes must be taken into account. As an example, if you are in the 35% tax bracket and inflation is 2.5%, your breakeven ROI will likely be in the range of 4.0%. In this example, if you are not getting better than a 4% ROI on your savings, your fund is not actually growing.

How Much is Enough Forecaster

www.retirementrocks.ca for .pdf copy or EXCEL model

Date: _____

First Step:	Estimate Your Expenses at Retirement (1ˢᵗ year)

First Step: **Estimate Your Expenses at Retirement (1ˢᵗ year)**

(1)   Your current monthly living expenses
       (from your Cash Flow Statement) $_____

(2)   Percentage of current living expenses (1)
       that you anticipate needing in retirement   _____%

(3)   An estimate of the annual inflation rate
                                                         _____%

(4)   Number of years in the future for calculation
       (how many years will it be until you retire)   _____

(5)   Factor from FV Table *($1 invested)*
       Lookup in tables using (3) and (4)   _____

(6)   Calculation of first year expenses at retirement

       (1) x (2) / 100 x (5) x 12 = $_____

Example using 2.5% inflation and 12 years until retirement:

$ 6,000 x 70 / 100 x 1.34489 x 12 = $ 67,782

How Much is Enough Forecaster

www.retirementrocks.ca for .pdf copy or EXCEL model

Second Step: Estimate Your Registered Savings at Retirement (RRSPs, Spousal RRSPs, LIRAs, DC Pensions)

(1)   Amount of registered savings (present value) (from your Net Worth Statement) $_____

(2)   Annual contribution to registered savings (average amount added each year) $_____

(3)   Average ROI on registered savings (expected annual growth rate percentage)   _____ %

(4)   Number of years in the future for calculation (how many years will it be until you retire)   _____

(5)   Factor from FV Table *($1 invested* – lump sum) Lookup in table using (3) and (4)   _____

(6)   Factor from FV Table *($1 invested each year)* Lookup in table using (3) and (4)   _____

(7)   Calculation of total registered savings at retirement

((1) x (5)) + ((2) x (6)) = $_____

Example using 6% ROI and 12 years until retirement:

($ 200,000 x 2.01220) + ($ 10,000 x 17.8821) = $ 581,261

How Much is Enough Forecaster

www.retirementrocks.ca for .pdf copy or EXCEL model

| Third Step: | Estimate Non-Registered Savings at Retirement (stock savings plans, investment accounts) |

(8)   Amount of your non-registered savings (present value)
         (from your Net Worth Statement) $_____

(9)   Annual contribution to non-registered savings
         (average amount added each year) $_____

(10)   Average ROI from non-registered savings
         (expected annual growth rate percentage)   _____ %

(11)   Number of years in the future for calculation
         (how many years will it be until you retire)   _____

(12)   Factor from FV Table *($1 invested* – lump sum)
         Lookup in table using (3) and (4)   _____

(13)   Factor from FV Table *($1 invested each year)*
         Lookup in table using (3) and (4)   _____

(14)   An estimate of taxes that will be payable
         (see Tables or consult Tax Accountant) $_____

(15)   Calculation of total non-registered savings at retirement

$$((8) \times (12)) + ((9) \times (13)) - (14) = \quad \$_____$$

Example using 6% ROI and 12 years until retirement:

($50,000 x 2.01220) + ($ 2,000 x 17.8821) − $ 50,000 = $ 86,374

How Much is Enough Forecaster

www.retirementrocks.ca for .pdf copy or EXCEL model

Fourth Step: Reasonableness Check – Is there Enough?

(1)   First year expenses at retirement
(from First Step, estimated expenses)   \$_____

(2)   Annual pension income
(company and government)   \$_____

(3)   Other income (estimated amount)
(annual income from all other sources)   \$_____

(4)   Reasonableness check calculation

$$((1) - (2) - (3)) \quad x \quad 20 \quad = \qquad \$_____$$

Example: (\$ 67,782 – \$ 30,000 – \$ 4,000) x 20 = \$ 675,640

(5)   Sum of registered and non-registered savings
(from 2nd Step (7) and 3rd Step (15))   \$_____

(6)   Excess or shortfall calculation (enough?)

$$(5) \quad - \quad (4) \quad = \qquad\qquad \$_____$$

Example: (\$ 581,261 + \$86,374) – \$ 675,640 =   - \$8,005

If the amount (6) is negative, then you likely need to save more and/or spend less.

If the amount (6) is positive, then you may be able to spend more and/or save less.

Net Worth Statement   Date: _____

www.retirementrocks.ca for .pdf copy or EXCEL model

	What I / We Own	(A)	What I / We Owe	(B)
	Asset	$ value	Liability	$ amount
1				
2				
3				
4				
5				
6				
7				
8				
9				
10				
11				
12				
13				
14				
15				
16				
17				
18				
19				
20				
	Totals:			

Net Worth: (A) _____ **minus (B)** _____ = _____

Cash Flow Statement   Date: _____

www.retirementrocks.ca for .pdf copy or EXCEL model

	Monthly Income	(A)	Monthly Spending	(B)
	Revenues	$ amount	Expenses	$ amount
1				
2				
3				
4				
5				
6				
7				
8				
9				
10				
11				
12				
13				
14				
15				
16				
17				
18				
19				
20				
	Totals:			

Cash Flow: (A) _____ minus (B) _____ = _____

Retirement Checklist

www.retirementrocks.ca for .pdf copy

√	My Financial "To Do" List	Date Completed
(__)	Complete and evaluate your net worth statement.	_____
(__)	Calculate your current living expenses.	_____
(__)	Create a debt re-payment plan.	_____
(__)	Clearly identify deductible and non-deductible interest expense.	_____
(__)	"Practise" living on retirement income for 6 months (to the extent practical).	_____
(__)	Create a purchasing plan for "big" toys and trips.	_____
(__)	Evaluate the retirement "pot" in each spouse's name.	_____
(__)	Draft income timeline for income-splitting review.	_____
(__)	Review asset mix and geographic distribution of your portfolio.	_____
(__)	Develop an investment policy statement.	_____
(__)	Evaluate tax efficiency of your portfolio.	_____
(__)	Order a current CPP statement of contributions.	_____
(__)	Regularly re-visit retirement calculation.	_____
(__)	Review and update your will.	_____
(__)	Draft or review Enduring Power of Attorney for Health and Property.	_____
(__)	Review insurance requirements.	_____

Financial Appendix

Financial Term Descriptions
Future Value (FV) Tables
LIF (LRIF) Payout Schedule
RRIF Minimum Withdrawals
Annuity Payout Chart
Income Tax Rate Chart
Taxation – Dividends, Interest, Capital Gains

LIFESTYLE | RELATIONSHIP | FINANCES

Financial Term Descriptions

The following are brief descriptions of abbreviations and terms (in alphabetical order) that are found in the Finances section.

In each case, refer to the appropriate chapter(s) and/or other information sources for more detail and practical application.

ANNUITY Types: Life and Term

Life: An insurance product involving deposit of a lump sum with an insurance company that features a predetermined periodic payout amount until the death of the annuitant.

Term: An insurance product involving deposit of a lump sum with an insurance company that guarantees a periodic payment of a predetermined amount for a fixed term.

ANNUITY Taxation: Prescribed and Non-prescribed

Prescribed: Investment interest is not taxed as earned. Instead, the total expected interest to be earned over the life of the contract is spread evenly over all payments.

Non-prescribed: Taxed using accrual taxation (taxed as earned). Income earned on the contract must be reported as taxpayer's income on each anniversary day of the policy.

CASH FLOW

A calculated measure of what cash comes in (revenues and incomes) less what cash goes out (expenses – what is spent). Cash Flow is generally calculated as a monthly amount.

CPP – Canada Pension Plan
Employers and individuals each pay into this program throughout all working years up to a set amount of maximum pensionable earnings. Eligibility begins at 60 years of age.

DB – Defined Benefit Pension Plan
These plans are administered by companies (usually larger organizations) and are based on a formula involving level of income, years of service, and employee age.

DC – Defined Contribution Pension Plan
Company contributions are based on a percentage of salary and this percentage may increase with years of service. Optional voluntary contributions may also be allowed.

EPA – Enduring Power of Attorney
A legal document that authorizes one or more persons to make decisions on behalf of another concerning assets (including financial), even in the event of loss of capacity.

GIS – Guaranteed Income Supplement
Federal Government program that provides assistance to eligible low-income Canadians. These types of programs are generally non-taxable and are means-tested annually.

LIF – Life Income Fund (same as LRIF in some provinces)
Converts LIRAs or LRSPs to income. Funds in LIRAs or LRSPs are not accessible (locked-in) until such time as conversion to a LIF is possible. Withdrawal limits apply.

LIRA – Locked In Retirement Account
Contains funds from a company pension plan when a pension plan member leaves the plan prior to retirement. Funds are available after retirement once converted to a LIF.

NET WORTH
A measure calculated by subtracting total liabilities (everything owed) from total assets (everything owned). For an individual, total assets are recorded at current market value.

OAS – Old Age Security
Income available to Canadian citizens and landed immigrants (65 or older). Qualification does not require having worked in Canada (means tested and subject to claw-back).

RCA – Retirement Compensation Agreement
An employer, a former employer, or an employee, contributes funds in trust to a custodian. The funds are distributed to the employee on, after, or in view of retirement.

RESP – Registered Education Savings Plan
A government-registered plan that allows savings for education to grow tax-free until the child (or children) named enrols in post-secondary education. A lifetime limit applies.

RRIF – Registered Retirement Income Fund (same as RIF)
Instead of putting money into an RRSP as savings, money is withdrawn as retirement income (a reverse RRSP). Withdrawal amounts have rules and minimum requirements.

RRSP – Registered Retirement Savings Plan (same as RSP)
A savings plan with tax-deductible contributions and tax-sheltered growth. Maximum annual contributions are based on income levels. Any withdrawal triggers taxation.

SA – Spousal Allowance
A program that provides some financial assistance to eligible low-income Canadians. These types of programs are generally non-taxable and are means-tested annually.

TFSA – Tax Free Savings Account
A savings account that can be open indefinitely, where contributions are NOT tax-deductible but growth, and withdrawals are tax-exempt. Annual maximums apply.

Future Value Factors ($1 invested – lump sum)

Table 1:   Use for existing savings investment growth

Year	1.0%	1.5%	2.0%	2.5%	3.0%
1	1.01000	1.01500	1.02000	1.02500	1.03000
2	1.02010	1.03022	1.04040	1.05063	1.06090
3	1.03030	1.04568	1.06121	1.07689	1.09273
4	1.04060	1.06136	1.08243	1.10381	1.12551
5	1.05101	1.07728	1.10408	1.13141	1.15927
6	1.06152	1.09344	1.12616	1.15969	1.19405
7	1.07214	1.10984	1.14869	1.18869	1.22987
8	1.08286	1.12649	1.17166	1.21840	1.26677
9	1.09369	1.14339	1.19509	1.24886	1.30477
10	1.10462	1.16054	1.21899	1.28008	1.34392
11	1.11567	1.17795	1.24337	1.31209	1.38423
12	1.12683	1.19562	1.26824	1.34489	1.42576
13	1.13809	1.21355	1.29361	1.37851	1.46853
14	1.14947	1.23176	1.31948	1.41297	1.51259
15	1.16097	1.25023	1.34587	1.44830	1.55797
16	1.17258	1.26899	1.37279	1.48451	1.60471
17	1.18430	1.28802	1.40024	1.52162	1.65285
18	1.19615	1.30734	1.42825	1.55966	1.70243
19	1.20811	1.32695	1.45681	1.59865	1.75351
20	1.22019	1.34686	1.48595	1.63862	1.80611
21	1.23239	1.36706	1.51567	1.67958	1.86029
25	1.28243	1.45095	1.64061	1.85394	2.09378
30	1.34785	1.56308	1.81136	2.09757	2.42726
40	1.48886	1.81402	2.20804	2.68506	3.26204

www.retirementrocks.ca for .pdf copy

Future Value Factors ($1 invested – lump sum)

Table 1:   Use for existing savings investment growth

Year	3.5%	4.0%	4.5%	5.0%
1	1.03500	1.04000	1.04500	1.05000
2	1.07123	1.08160	1.09203	1.10250
3	1.10872	1.12486	1.14117	1.15763
4	1.14752	1.16986	1.19252	1.21551
5	1.18769	1.21665	1.24618	1.27628
6	1.22926	1.26532	1.30226	1.34010
7	1.27228	1.31593	1.36086	1.40710
8	1.31681	1.36857	1.42210	1.47746
9	1.36290	1.42331	1.48610	1.55133
10	1.41060	1.48024	1.55297	1.62889
11	1.45997	1.53945	1.62285	1.71034
12	1.51107	1.60103	1.69588	1.79586
13	1.56396	1.66507	1.77220	1.88565
14	1.61869	1.73168	1.85194	1.97993
15	1.67535	1.80094	1.93528	2.07893
16	1.73399	1.87298	2.02237	2.18287
17	1.79468	1.94790	2.11338	2.29202
18	1.85749	2.02582	2.20848	2.40662
19	1.92250	2.10685	2.30786	2.52695
20	1.98979	2.19112	2.41171	2.65330
21	2.05943	2.27877	2.52024	2.78596
25	2.36324	2.66584	3.00543	3.38635
30	2.80679	3.24340	3.74532	4.32194
40	13.95926	4.80102	5.81636	7.03999

www.retirementrocks.ca for .pdf copy

Future Value Factors ($1 invested – lump sum)

Table 1:   Use for existing savings investment growth

Year	5.5%	6.0%	7.0%	8.0%	9.0%
1	1.05500	1.06000	1.07000	1.08000	1.09000
2	1.11303	1.12360	1.14490	1.16640	1.18810
3	1.17424	1.19102	1.22504	1.25971	1.29503
4	1.23882	1.26248	1.31080	1.36049	1.41158
5	1.30696	1.33823	1.40255	1.46933	1.53862
6	1.37884	1.41852	1.50073	1.58687	1.67710
7	1.45468	1.50363	1.60578	1.71382	1.82804
8	1.53469	1.59385	1.71819	1.85093	1.99256
9	1.61909	1.68948	1.83846	1.99900	2.17189
10	1.70814	1.79085	1.96715	2.15892	2.36736
11	1.80209	1.89830	2.10485	2.33164	2.58043
12	1.90121	2.01220	2.25219	2.51817	2.81266
13	2.00577	2.13293	2.40985	2.71962	3.06580
14	2.11609	2.26090	2.57853	2.93719	3.34173
15	2.23248	2.39656	2.75903	3.17217	3.64248
16	2.35526	2.54035	2.95216	3.42594	3.97031
17	2.48480	2.69277	3.15882	3.70002	4.32763
18	2.62147	2.85434	3.37993	3.99602	4.71712
19	2.76565	3.02560	3.61653	4.31570	5.14166
20	2.91776	3.20714	3.86968	4.66096	5.60441
21	3.07823	3.39956	4.14056	5.03383	6.10881
25	3.81339	4.29187	5.42743	6.84848	8.62308
30	4.98395	5.74349	7.61226	10.06266	13.26768
40	8.51331	10.28572	14.97446	21.72452	31.40942

www.retirementrocks.ca for .pdf copy

Future Value Factors ($1 invested each year)

Table 2:   Use for annual contribution investment growth

Year	1.0%	1.5%	2.0%	2.5%	3.0%
1	1.0100	1.0150	1.0200	1.0250	1.0300
2	2.0301	2.0452	2.0604	2.0756	2.0909
3	3.0604	3.0909	3.1216	3.1525	3.1836
4	4.1010	4.1523	4.2040	4.2563	4.3091
5	5.1520	5.2296	5.3081	5.3877	5.4684
6	6.2135	6.3230	6.4343	6.5474	6.6625
7	7.2857	7.4328	7.5830	7.7361	7.8923
8	8.3685	8.5593	8.7546	8.9545	9.1591
9	9.4622	9.7027	9.9497	10.2034	10.4639
10	10.5668	10.8633	11.1687	11.4835	11.8078
11	11.6825	12.0412	12.4121	12.7956	13.1920
12	12.8093	13.2368	13.6803	14.1404	14.6178
13	13.9474	14.4504	14.9739	15.5190	16.0863
14	15.0969	15.6821	16.2934	16.9319	17.5989
15	16.2579	16.9324	17.6393	18.3802	19.1569
16	17.4304	18.2014	19.0121	19.8647	20.7616
17	18.6147	19.4894	20.4123	21.3863	22.4144
18	19.8109	20.7967	21.8406	22.9460	24.1169
19	21.0190	22.1237	23.2974	24.5447	25.8704
20	22.2392	23.4705	24.7833	26.1833	27.6765
21	23.4716	24.8376	26.2990	27.8629	29.5368
25	28.5256	30.5140	32.6709	35.0117	37.5530
30	35.1327	38.1018	41.3794	45.0003	49.0027
40	49.3752	55.0819	61.6100	69.0876	77.6633

www.retirementrocks.ca for .pdf copy

Future Value Factors ($1 invested each year)

Table 2: Use for annual contribution investment growth

Year	3.5%	4.0%	4.5%	5.0%
1	1.0350	1.0400	1.0450	1.0500
2	2.1062	2.1216	2.1370	2.1525
3	3.2149	3.2465	3.2782	3.3101
4	4.3625	4.4163	4.4707	4.5256
5	5.5502	5.6330	5.7169	5.8019
6	6.7794	6.8983	7.0192	7.1420
7	8.0517	8.2142	8.3800	8.5491
8	9.3685	9.5828	9.8021	10.0266
9	10.7314	11.0061	11.2882	11.5779
10	12.1420	12.4864	12.8412	13.2068
11	13.6020	14.0258	14.4640	14.9171
12	15.1130	15.6268	16.1599	16.7130
13	16.6770	17.2919	17.9321	18.5986
14	18.2957	19.0236	19.7841	20.5786
15	19.9710	20.8245	21.7193	22.6575
16	21.7050	22.6975	23.7417	24.8404
17	23.4997	24.6454	25.8551	27.1324
18	25.3572	26.6712	28.0636	29.5390
19	27.2797	28.7781	30.3714	32.0660
20	29.2695	30.9692	32.7831	34.7193
21	31.3289	33.2480	35.3034	37.5052
25	40.3131	43.3117	46.5706	50.1135
30	53.4295	58.3283	63.7524	69.7608
40	87.5095	98.8265	111.8467	126.8398

www.retirementrocks.ca for .pdf copy

Future Value Factors ($1 invested each year)

Table 2:   Use for annual contribution investment growth

Year	5.5%	6.0%	7.0%	8.0%	9.0%
1	1.0550	1.0600	1.0700	1.0800	1.0900
2	2.1680	2.1836	2.2149	2.2464	2.2781
3	3.3423	3.3746	3.4399	3.5061	3.5731
4	4.5811	4.6371	4.7507	4.8666	4.9847
5	5.8881	5.9753	6.1533	6.3359	6.5233
6	7.2669	7.3938	7.6540	7.9228	8.2004
7	8.7216	8.8975	9.2598	9.6366	10.0285
8	10.2563	10.4913	10.9780	11.4876	12.0210
9	11.8754	12.1808	12.8164	13.4866	14.1929
10	13.5835	13.9716	14.7836	15.6455	16.5603
11	15.3856	15.8699	16.8885	17.9771	19.1407
12	17.2868	17.8821	19.1406	20.4953	21.9534
13	19.2926	20.0151	21.5505	23.2149	25.0192
14	21.4087	22.2760	24.1290	26.1521	28.3609
15	23.6411	24.6725	26.8881	29.3243	32.0034
16	25.9964	27.2129	29.8402	32.7502	35.9737
17	28.4812	29.9057	32.9990	36.4502	40.3013
18	31.1027	32.7600	36.3790	40.4463	45.0185
19	33.8683	35.7856	39.9955	44.7620	50.1601
20	36.7861	38.9927	43.8652	49.4229	55.7645
21	39.8643	42.3923	48.0057	54.4568	61.8733
25	53.9660	58.1564	67.6765	78.9544	92.3240
30	76.4194	83.8017	101.0730	122.3459	148.5752
40	144.1189	164.0477	213.6096	279.7810	368.2919

www.retirementrocks.ca for .pdf copy

LIF Payout Schedule (2009)

Column	Description
A	Years of age as of January 1, 2009
B	Minimum withdrawal (non-qualified)
C	Maximum withdrawal (ON, SK, NB, NL)
D	Maximum withdrawal (QC, MB, NS, BC)
E	Maximum withdrawal for Federal (PBSA)
F	Maximum withdrawal (AB)

A	B	C	D	E	F
50	2.50%	6.27%	6.10%	5.24%	6.51%
51	2.56%	6.31%	6.10%	5.28%	6.57%
52	2.63%	6.35%	6.10%	5.32%	6.63%
53	2.70%	6.40%	6.10%	5.36%	6.70%
54	2.78%	6.45%	6.10%	5.41%	6.77%
55	2.86%	6.51%	6.40%	5.46%	6.85%
56	2.94%	6.57%	6.50%	5.52%	6.94%
57	3.03%	6.63%	6.50%	5.58%	7.04%
58	3.13%	6.70%	6.60%	5.65%	7.14%
59	3.23%	6.77%	6.70%	5.71%	7.26%
60	3.33%	6.85%	6.70%	5.79%	7.38%
61	3.45%	6.94%	6.80%	5.87%	7.52%
62	3.57%	7.04%	6.90%	5.96%	7.67%

A	B	C	D	E	F
63	3.70%	7.14%	7.00%	6.06%	7.83%
64	3.85%	7.26%	7.10%	6.17%	8.02%
65	4.00%	7.38%	7.20%	6.29%	8.22%
66	4.17%	7.52%	7.30%	6.42%	8.45%
67	4.35%	7.67%	7.40%	6.57%	8.71%
68	4.55%	7.83%	7.60%	6.73%	9.00%
69	4.76%	8.02%	7.70%	6.92%	9.34%
70	5.00%	8.22%	7.90%	7.12%	9.71%
71	7.38%	8.45%	8.10%	7.35%	10.15%
72	7.48%	8.71%	8.30%	7.61%	10.66%
73	7.59%	9.00%	8.50%	7.91%	11.25%
74	7.71%	9.34%	8.80%	8.25%	11.96%
75	7.85%	9.71%	9.10%	8.65%	12.82%
76	7.99%	10.15%	9.40%	9.10%	13.87%
77	8.15%	10.66%	9.80%	9.63%	15.19%
78	8.33%	11.25%	10.30%	10.25%	16.90%
79	8.53%	11.96%	10.80%	10.98%	19.19%
80	8.75%	12.82%	11.50%	11.85%	22.40%
81	8.99%	13.87%	12.10%	12.93%	27.23%
82	9.27%	15.19%	12.90%	14.28%	35.29%
83	9.58%	16.90%	13.80%	16.02%	51.46%
84	9.93%	19.19%	14.80%	18.34%	100.00%
85	10.33%	22.40%	16.00%	21.60%	100.00%

A	B	C	D	E	F
86	10.79%	27.23%	17.30%	26.49%	100.00%
87	11.33%	35.29%	18.90%	34.65%	100.00%
88	11.96%	51.46%	20.00%	50.98%	100.00%
89	12.71%	100.00%	20.00%	100.00%	100.00%
90	13.62%	100.00%	20.00%	100.00%	100.00%
91	14.73%	100.00%	20.00%	100.00%	100.00%
92	16.12%	100.00%	20.00%	100.00%	100.00%
93	17.92%	100.00%	20.00%	100.00%	100.00%
94 and above	20.00%	100.00%	20.00%	100.00%	100.00%

Column	Description
A	Years of age as of January 1, 2009
B	Minimum withdrawal (non-qualified)
C	Maximum withdrawal (ON, SK, NB, NL)
D	Maximum withdrawal (QC, MB, NS, BC)
E	Maximum withdrawal for Federal (PBSA)
F	Maximum withdrawal (AB)

RRIF Minimum Withdrawals (2009)

Formula before age 71 =

(market value on Jan. 1) divided by (90 minus Jan. 1 age)

Age	General	Qualifying RRIF (established before 1993)
71	7.38	5.26
72	7.48	5.56
73	7.59	5.88
74	7.71	6.25
75	7.85	6.67
76	7.99	7.14
77	8.15	7.69
78	8.33	8.33
79	8.53	8.53
80	8.75	8.75
81	8.99	8.99
82	9.27	9.27
83	9.58	9.58
84	9.93	9.93
85	10.33	10.33
86	10.79	10.79
87	11.33	11.33
88	11.96	11.96
89	12.71	12.71
90	13.62	13.62
91	14.73	14.73
92	16.12	16.12
93	17.92	17.92
94	20.00	20.00
94+	20.00	20.00

Annuity Payout Chart - from www.investored.ca (2009)

The chart below is an example of what purchasing an annuity means in terms of monthly income in retirement. It is based on an initial investment of $100,000 in a single straight life annuity, and shows how income may drop as extra options are added.

Type of Annuity	What it's Designed to do	Sample Monthly Annuity Income
Straight life	Provides you with income for life	$650
Life plus five-year guarantee	Provides you with income for life. Guarantees 60 payments to your estate in case you die within the first five years of your contract	$640
Life plus 10-year guarantee	Provides you with income for life. Guarantees 120 payments to your estate in case you die within the first 10 years of your contract	$620
Life plus joint-and-last-survivor	Provides income for life for you and your spouse. Payments stop when both of you have died	$500
Indexed life annuity	Provides income for life. Payments increase with inflation to maintain your buying power Sample income is the initial income which will increase with inflation.	$400

Income Tax Rate Chart
From Canada Revenue Agency – www.cra.gc.ca

Federal tax rates for 2009

- = 15% **on the first** $38,832 of taxable income

- + 22% **on the next** $38,832 of taxable income (on the portion of taxable income between $38,832 and $77,664)

- + 26% **on the next** $48,600 of taxable income (on the portion of taxable income between $77,664 and $126,264)

- + 29% of taxable income **over** $126,264

Note:

For 2009, the federal budget included an increase to the upper taxable income thresholds of the 15% and 22% tax brackets. For more information about these changes, see the questions and answers in CRA 2009 Budget News.

Provincial/Territorial tax rates for 2009

Under the current tax on income method, tax for all provinces (except Quebec) and territories is calculated the same way as federal tax. Form 428 is used to calculate this provincial or territorial tax. Provincial or territorial specific non-refundable tax credits are also calculated on Form 428. For complete details, see the *Provincial or Territorial information and forms* in your 2009 tax package.

Provincial / Territorial tax rates (combined chart)	
Provinces & Territories	**Rate(s)**
Newfoundland and Labrador	7.7% on the first $31,061 of taxable income, + 12.8% on the next $31,060, + 15.5% on the amount over $62,121
Prince Edward Island	9.8% on the first $31,984 of taxable income, + 13.8% on the next $31,985, + 16.7% on the amount over $63,969
Nova Scotia	8.79% on the first $29,590 of taxable income, + 14.95% on the next $29,590, +16.67% on the next $33,820 + 17.5% on the amount over $93,000
New Brunswick	10.12% on the first $35,707 of taxable income, + 15.48% on the next $35,708, + 16.8% on the next $44,690, + 17.95% on the amount over $116,105
Quebec	Contact Revenu Québec
Ontario	6.05% on the first $36,848 of taxable income, + 9.15% on the next $36,850, + 11.16% on the amount over $73,698

Manitoba	10.8% on the first $31,000 of taxable income, + 12.75% on the next $36,000, + 17.4% on the amount over $67,000
Saskatchewan	11% on the first $40,113 of taxable income, + 13% on the next $74,497, + 15% on the amount over $114,610
Alberta	10% of taxable income
British Columbia	5.06% on the first $35,716 of taxable income, + 7.7% on the next $35,717, + 10.5% on the next $10,581, + 12.29% on the next $17,574, + 14.7% on the amount over $99,588
Yukon	7.04% on the first $38,832 of taxable income, + 9.68% on the next $38,832, + 11.44% on the next $48,600, + 12.76% on the amount over $126,264
Northwest Territories	5.9% on the first $36,885 of taxable income, + 8.6% on the next $36,887, + 12.2% on the next $46,164, + 14.05% on the amount over $119,936
Nunavut	4% on the first $38,832 of taxable income, + 7% on the next $38,832, + 9% on the next $48,600, + 11.5% on the amount over $126,264

Taxation – Interest, Dividends, and Capital Gains
From Manulife Investments (2008)

Top Marginal Tax Rates %	BC	AB	SK	MB	ON	QC	NB
Interest / other income	43.70	39.00	44.00	46.40	46.41	48.22	46.95
Capital Gains	21.85	19.50	22.00	23.20	23.21	24.11	23.48
Eligible Dividends	18.47	16.00	20.35	23.83	23.96	29.69	23.18
Ineligible Dividends	31.58	26.46	30.83	37.40	31.34	36.35	35.40

Top Marginal Tax Rates %	NS	PE	NL	YK	NT	NU	non-res.
Interest / other income	48.25	47.37	45.00	42.40	43.05	40.50	42.92
Capital Gains	24.13	23.69	22.50	21.20	21.53	20.25	21.46
Eligible Dividends	28.35	24.44	28.11	17.23	18.25	22.24	21.53
Ineligible Dividends	33.06	33.61	33.33	30.49	29.65	28.96	28.98

Note: Refer to the section on Personal Savings and Investments (Tax Efficient Investing) for an explanation of how interest, dividends, and capital gains are taxed differently.

Reference and Suggested Reading

General

Biscott, Lynn. *The Boomers Retire – A Guide for Financial Advisors and Their Clients.* Toronto: Thomson Carswell, 2008

Bolles, R.N. & Nelson, J.E. *What Color is Your Parachute? For Retirement.* Berklely: Ten Speed Press, 2007

Borchard, David C. *The Joy of Retirement.* New York: AMACOM, 2008

Cooper, Dr. Sherry. *The New Retirement: How It Will Change Your Future.* Toronto: Viking Canada, 2008

Covey, Stephen R. *First Things First.* New York: Simon & Schuster, 1995

Covey, Stephen R. *The 7 Habits of Highly Effective People.* New York: Simon & Schuster, 1990

Hansen, Mark V. & Linkletter, Art. *How to Make the Rest of Your Life the Best of Your Life.* Nashville: Thomas Nelson, Inc., 2006

Hovanec, M. & Shilton, E. *Redefining Retirement New Realities for Boomer Women.* Toronto: Second Story Press, 2007

Vandervelde, Maryanne. *Retirement For Two.* New York: Bantam Dell, 2005

Zelinski, Ernie J. *The Joy of Not Working A Book for The Retired, Unemployed and Overworked*. Berkeley: Ten Speed Press, 2003

Zoomer Magazine published 9 times per year by ZoomerMedia Limited. Canadian magazine dealing with health, lifestyle, relationship issues for men and women 45 and up.

Lifestyle

Irvine, David. *Simple Living In A Complex World: A Guide To Balancing Life's Achievements*. Toronto: John Wiley & Sons Canada Ltd, 2004.

Schultz, Patricia. *1,000 Places to See Before You Die*. New York: Workman Publishing, 2003

Wallace, Danny. *The Yes Man*. New York: SSE a division of Simon & Schuster, Inc., 2008

www.centreforinspiredliving.com

Relationships

Nelson, Noelle C. *Your Man Is Wonderful*. New York: Free Press, division of Simon & Schuster, Inc., 2009

Mrakman, H.J., Stanley, S.M., & Blumberg. *Fighting For Your Marriage*. San Francisco: Jossey-Bass by John Wiley & Sons, Inc., 2001

Hendrix, Harville. *Getting the Love You Want A Guide For Couples*. New York: HarperCollins Publishers, 1990.

Nemzoff, Ruth. *Don't Bite Your Tongue – How to Foster Rewarding Relationships with Your Adult Children*. New York: Palgrave Macmillan, 2008

Finances

Bach, David. *Start Late, Finish Rich: A No-fail Plan for Achieving Financial Freedom At Any Age*. Doubleday Canada, 2005

Bach, David. *Fight For Your Money How to Stop Getting Ripped Off and Save a Fortune*. Doubleday Canada, 2009

MoneySense a Canadian financial magazine published 6 times per year by Rogers Media. www.moneysense.ca

By using recycled stock to print this book, the following was saved:

4.25
Trees

2,549
Gallons of Water

524lbs
Air emissions

270lbs
solid waste